# SELF-WORKING
# HANDKERCHIEF
# MAGIC

## 61 Foolproof Tricks

by Karl Fulves

*With 509 Illustrations by*
*Joseph K. Schmidt*

DOVER PUBLICATIONS, INC.
*New York*

*Self-Working Handkerchief Magic: 61 Foolproof Tricks* is a new
work, first published by Dover Publications, Inc., in 1988.

Manufactured in the United States of America
Dover Publications, Inc., 31 East 2nd Street, Mineola, N.Y.
11501

*Library of Congress Cataloging-in-Publication Data*

Fulves, Karl.
  Self-working handkerchief magic.

  1. Tricks. 2. Handkerchiefs. I. Title.
GV1559.F835 1988      793.8       88-11859
ISBN 0-486-25694-4 (pbk.)

# Introduction

Handkerchief tricks are a graceful branch of magic; if one wants to start a magic act with a dramatic visual effect, there is none better than those offered by handkerchief tricks. In platform or stage magic it is particularly important to please the eye. In this regard handkerchief tricks are ideal. Many professional acts feature handkerchief effects because they embody the essence of sophisticated magic.

Handkerchief magic is a comparatively recent addition to the art. Professor Hoffmann observed: "Until Bautier de Kolta showed the way, no one seems to have appreciated the intrinsic capabilities of the silk handkerchief as a magical property." Since de Kolta's time, handkerchief magic has seen rapid development. Magicians have perfected spectacular acts that feature handkerchief tricks only.

There are many excellent handkerchief tricks that rely on sleight of hand, custom apparatus or special gimmicks to work. They are outside the scope of this book. For important background on such material, consult Hugard's *Handkerchief Magic* (Dover, ISBN 0-486-20734-X). The earliest, and still the most extensive, treatment of mechanical handkerchief gimmicks can be found in Hoffmann's *Later Magic*.

The present book is a collection of handkerchief tricks that are easy to perform. Most can be done on the spur of the moment. A few require simple apparatus constructed from cardboard or paper. The apparatus for all of the tricks in this book will fit into a slender briefcase, yet the tricks are colorful and most can be performed either close-up or from the stage.

Although most of these tricks are simple, the key to success is to learn them thoroughly so they can be performed smoothly. And it should be noted that, although the directions given here seem to imply that the magician is a man (the traditional manner for giving directions in magic), they are, of course, also intended to be used by women.

For background on the material in the following pages I am indebted to Howard Wurst. The lucid artwork is by the eminent magic artist Joseph K. Schmidt.

KARL FULVES

# Contents

# THE BASICS

Almost without exception, any trick in this book is one that can be done with handkerchiefs made from cotton, silk or synthetics. In some cases cotton or silk is specified, but you may find that a synthetic blend will work as well. A few of the tricks can even be done with good-quality paper napkins.

Silk handkerchiefs (unlike cotton or synthetics) can be compressed into a small space. Magic-supply houses and shops that sell silk can provide handkerchiefs made from pure silk. The investment in pure silk handkerchiefs will pay dividends over the long run; properly handled and cared for, silk handkerchiefs will last for decades.

In magician's parlance, a handkerchief made from silk is referred to simply as "a silk." In this book, when reference is made to an 18″ silk, for example, it means a silk handkerchief measuring 18″ on a side, Figure 1. The shop from which you purchase silks will tell you how to care for them. Heat and light tend to fade the colors and cause silk to lose its springiness, so it is best to store silks by keeping them flat and unfolded in a cool, dark place.

Handkerchiefs can be introduced into a magic act in a number of ways. For example, use a handkerchief to cover a piece of apparatus. Uncover the apparatus as if to perform a trick with it. Then seem to

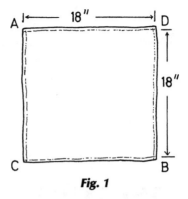

**Fig. 1**

remember a trick you once learned with a handkerchief. Do the trick, start to put the handkerchief aside, then appear to recall another handkerchief trick. Do that trick, then another and another, never quite getting around to the trick with the apparatus.

In some tricks in this book, the corners of the handkerchief will be referred to by letters of the alphabet, an example of which is shown in Figure 1. When learning the trick, you may wish to label the corners using a pencil lightly. When you have mastered the trick, you can erase the pencil writing.

Although the sizes of handkerchiefs are specified in many of the tricks in this book, you may find that a handkerchief of smaller or larger size is better suited to your way of working. Also keep in mind that it does make a difference whether a handkerchief is made of cotton, silk or some other material. Try different materials and different sizes to find the combination that is best for your individual style. Remember that, unlike playing cards, handkerchiefs are not manufactured to a common standard. The ideal handkerchief is the one you feel most comfortable with.

# QUICK TRICKS

A good magic trick should have a clear plot, one that the audience finds easy to follow. The tricks in this chapter use simple props to produce visual magic.

## 1. Threading the Needle

This trick is perhaps one of the best-known effects with a handkerchief, but the correct handling is little known. Use a 27″ handkerchief for maximum visibility. A silk handkerchief works best, but the stunt will work with handkerchiefs made from other materials.

METHOD: Hold the handkerchief by diagonally opposite corners, as shown in Figure 2. Twirl the lower end in circular fashion in the direction of the arrow in Figure 2. Make sure you twirl the lower end only. If you twirl both ends, the handkerchief will quickly unfurl. Continue twirling the handkerchief until it is twisted rope fashion, Figure 3.

Place end A between the right thumb and first finger, Figure 4. The palm-down left hand then grasps the center of the handkerchief,

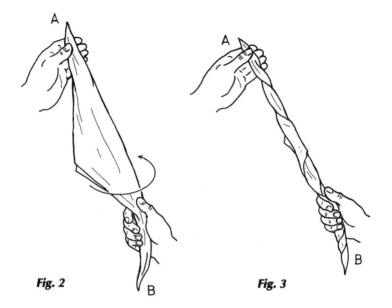

Fig. 2    Fig. 3

Figure 5. Release end A. Then bring end B up to the position shown in Figure 6. Wrap the upper part of the handkerchief around the left thumb, Figures 7 and 8.

Now bring end B between the left second and third fingers, Figure 9. Up to this point the right hand has not let go of end B. This means that the handling depicted in Figures 2 through 9 can be done in one smooth continuous motion.

When you reach the point shown in Figure 9, you have formed a loop above the left thumb. Release the right hand's grip on end B. Point to the loop with the right first finger and say, "This is the eye of the needle. The problem is to thread this end through the needle."

As you say, ". . . this end," grasp end A with the palm-up right hand, Figure 10, and bring it forward so that the strand of material grasped by the right hand can move to a position above the left first finger, Figure 11.

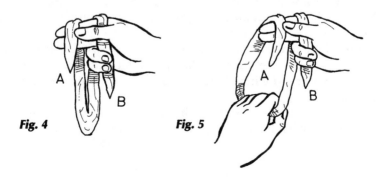

Fig. 4    Fig. 5

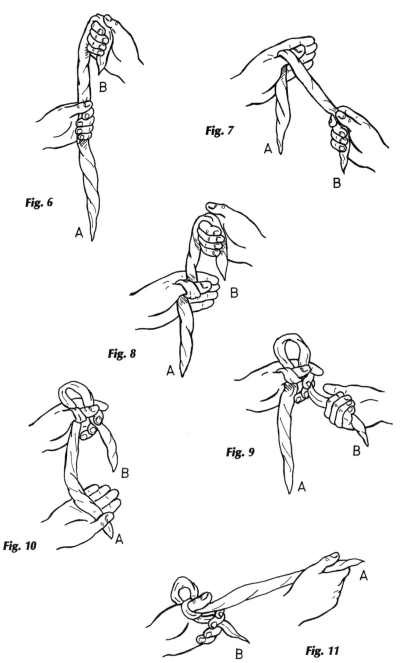

**Fig. 6**

**Fig. 7**

**Fig. 8**

**Fig. 9**

**Fig. 10**

**Fig. 11**

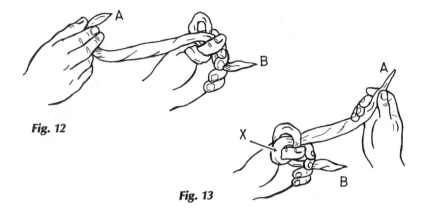

**Fig. 12**

**Fig. 13**

Draw end A back behind the left hand, Figure 12. Poke end A at the eye of the needle a few times. Then bring end A back to the position shown in Figure 12 again. Say, "To make it harder, I'll try to thread the needle without letting go of the end."

Quickly bring end A to the position shown in Figure 13, pulling the handkerchief taut as you do so. It appears as if you have threaded end A through the loop. You have actually pulled the center of the handkerchief up into the loop. To facilitate this action, when the right hand reaches the position shown in Figure 12, in preparation for the quick, lunging motion to the right, loosen the left hand's grip on the center of the handkerchief.

When bringing the handkerchief to the position shown in Figure 13, make sure the right hand is either above or below the left hand. This insures that the audience gets a clear view of the loop. To finish the stunt, release the right hand's grip on end A. Then grip the handkerchief at point X in Figure 13 and pull the handkerchief out of the loop. This strengthens the illusion that you really did thread the loop.

## 2.   Comedy Production

If you do a trick in which a pencil is used, you can produce the pencil in an amusing way. The magician drapes a handkerchief over his empty left hand. Instantly an object pops up under the handkerchief.

The magician removes the handkerchief to reveal—his first finger, Figure 22. The handkerchief is then turned over, revealing the pencil.

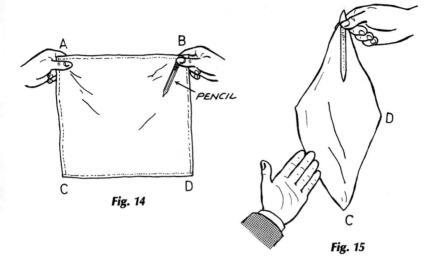

Fig. 14

Fig. 15

METHOD: Use an opaque 18″ handkerchief and a pencil about 5″ long. At the start have the apparatus in a briefcase.

When you are ready to present the routine, grasp the handkerchief at the upper corners. Hold the pencil behind the handkerchief with the right thumb. When the apparatus is in the correct position, lift it out of the briefcase and display the handkerchief, Figure 14.

Release the left hand's grip on the handkerchief. Turn the left hand palm up and bring it to the center of the handkerchief, Figure 15. Drape the handkerchief over the left hand, Figure 16. Note that the pencil is hidden by the handkerchief and also by the left arm.

Push the pencil upward so it is above the corner of the handkerchief, Figure 17. Curl the left fingers inward, clipping the pencil through the handkerchief with the left third finger. This is shown in

Fig. 16

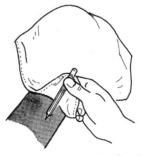

Fig. 17

*Fig. 18*

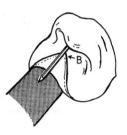

*Fig. 19*

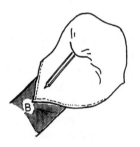

*Fig. 20*

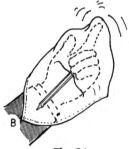

*Fig. 21*

*Fig. 22*

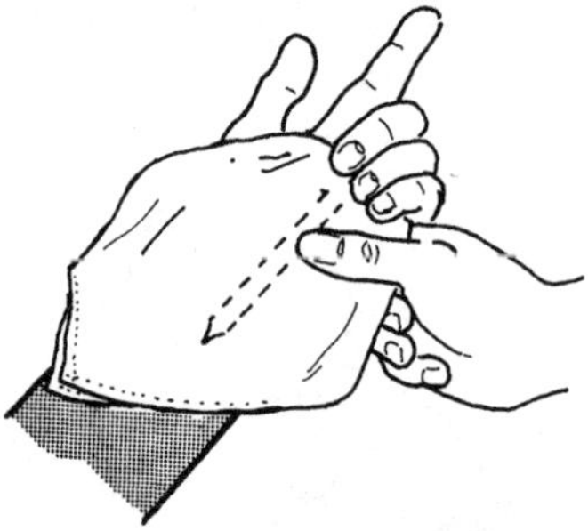

*Fig. 23*

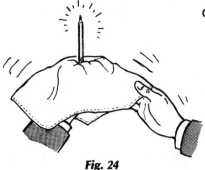

**Fig. 24**

Figure 18, with the handkerchief removed for clarity. The actual situation is indicated in Figure 19.

The right hand pulls corner B out from under the handkerchief so that corner B lies against the left arm, Figure 20. It should appear as though you are making slight adjustments to the position of the handkerchief. Announce that you will make an amazing production. Snap the right fingers. Then quickly bring the left first finger to a vertical position under the handkerchief, Figure 21.

Since the handkerchief is opaque, the audience doesn't know what object you have produced. Pause for a second to let the audience's interest focus on the left hand, then lift up the forward corner of the handkerchief (corner C) with the right hand and bring it back onto the left arm, Figure 22, to reveal that you have produced your first finger.

Wiggle the first finger as you say, "A moving finger. As you know, the moving finger writes." Pause here, then add, "And this is what it writes with."

As you speak, grasp the center of the handkerchief and the pencil with the right hand, Figure 23, and adjust the position so that the pencil is now firmly grasped by the left middle finger.

Then lift off the upper layer of the handkerchief with the right hand to reveal the pencil, Figure 24. The handkerchief can now be used for a trick like "General Rise" (No. 21) where the pencil is made to penetrate the handkerchief magically.

## 3.  A Glass of Helium

The magician explains that he has a glass of helium that is covered so the lighter-than-air gas does not evaporate. A pencil or pen is pushed down into the center of the glass, Figure 25. Instantly the pen shoots several feet in the air, Figure 26. Similarly, other objects, such as coins, rings, pingpong balls and match packets, become airborne after being immersed in helium.

METHOD: This trick was devised by the author. The secret is that a rubber band is placed around the glass beforehand, Figure 27. The glass is then covered with an opaque handkerchief.

To present the trick, pick up the handkerchief-covered glass with the left hand. Place the right hand under the handkerchief and grasp the glass. The left hand pushes a pen down into the center of the handkerchief, Figure 25, so that the end of the pen rests on the rubber band. This has the effect of pushing the rubber band downward. When the left hand releases the pen, the pen will shoot upward as shown in Figure 26.

Straighten the handkerchief so it lies smoothly over the top of the glass. Pick up another small object, such as a 6″ ruler. Push it down into the center of the handkerchief, but do not engage the rubber band. Release the ruler. Nothing happens. Remove the ruler. Shake the glass as if to stir up the helium. Then push the ruler down into the glass so it engages the rubber band. Release the ruler and it will jump into the air.

To finish so the apparatus can be examined, curl the right third and fourth fingers inward, Figure 28, so they touch the portion of the rubber band at the base of the glass. Force the rubber band back so it slides off the bottom of the glass. It is held in place by the right thumb, Figure 29. Gently ease the thumb back so the rubber band will jump up to the top of the glass, where there it can be picked off by the left thumb and first finger, Figure 30, as the handkerchief is whisked away from the glass. Turn the glass upside down and shake it, remarking that the helium has vanished.

The trick can end on an unexpected note. Get a bright red handkerchief, fold it in half and roll it into a cylinder. Drop it into the glass as shown in Figure 31. It should just fill the inside of the glass to a point about ½″ from the top. At a distance it will look as if the glass is filled with a liquid.

With the red silk in place, prepare the glass as shown in Figure 27. Perform the routine as written above, using a white opaque handkerchief to cover the glass. When you remove the white handkerchief, it appears as though you have a glass of liquid. Say, "It looks like tomato juice, but the helium has evaporated, leaving me with just this."

Slowly draw the red silk out of the glass. From the audience view it will appear as if a glass of red liquid has been transformed into a red silk handkerchief.

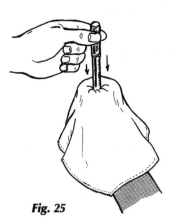

**Fig. 25**

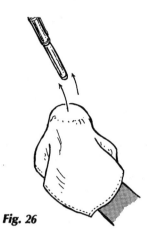

**Fig. 26**

RUBBER BAND

**Fig. 27**

**Fig. 28**

**Fig. 29**

**Fig. 30**

SILK

**Fig. 31**

## 4.  The Holdup

The story is told of the time the magician was walking home late one night when he was accosted by a thief who demanded his valuables. The magician had no money or credit cards, but did have a gold pen and pencil that had been in the family for years.

The thief took the pen and pencil, put them into a cloth bag and disappeared into the night. The magician reenacts the theft by dropping a pen and pencil into an impromptu handkerchief bag.

"When the thief got several blocks away, he stopped to examine his ill-gotten gains. He was surprised to discover that he had gotten nothing." The magician shakes open the handkerchief to show it empty. The pen and pencil are then produced from a paper bag.

METHOD: Place an 18″ handkerchief flat on the table, Figure 32. Fold the bottom up to the top, Figure 33. Then fold the right half over onto the left, Figure 34, to form an impromptu handkerchief bag.

Grasp the bag by the upper corners with the left hand, Figure 35. A pen is placed into the compartment nearest the performer's body, Figure 35. The audience does not know that this compartment of the bag is open at the left. It is thus an easy matter to slip the pen into the left jacket sleeve, as indicated in Figure 36.

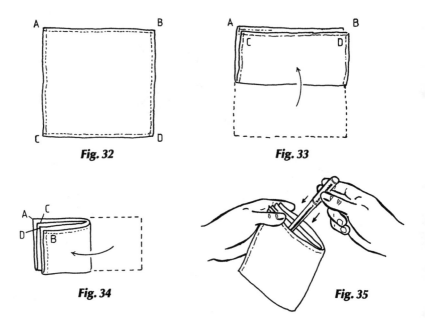

Fig. 32

Fig. 33

Fig. 34

Fig. 35

Although the secret removal of the pen is well covered by the handkerchief bag, you can create more cover by making sure the back of the right hand is kept toward the audience. A top view showing the correct position of the hands is given in Figure 37. When practicing the handling in front of a mirror, try it first facing front, then facing slightly left and slightly right. Note which position creates the most cover and stand that way when performing the trick for your audience.

After the pen has been secretly placed in the sleeve, repeat the above handling with a pencil, openly placing it into the handkerchief bag but secretly feeding it into the left jacket sleeve. Grasp the handkerchief bag at the top with the right hand. Then shake it out to show that the pen and pencil have vanished.

There are many ways to produce the pen and pencil again. One method is to have an open paper bag on the table. In the bottom of the bag is a folded napkin or towel that acts as a cushion. Lower the left hand into the bag, allowing the pen and pencil to slide out of the sleeve, Figure 37-A. They will fall noiselessly to the bottom of the bag.

Pretend to search for the pen and pencil with the left hand, remove the left hand, act puzzled, then reach into the bag with the right hand and remove the pen and pencil.

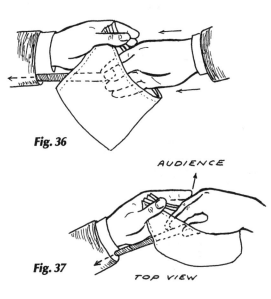

**Fig. 36**

AUDIENCE

**Fig. 37**

TOP VIEW

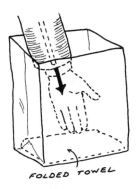

FOLDED TOWEL

**Fig. 37-A**

## 5.  Mystery Ring

The ends of a shoelace or piece of string are knotted together. The string is placed under a handkerchief. The magician borrows a ring or plastic bracelet. He causes the ring to become linked onto the string, Figure 38. When the ends of the string are pulled, the ring comes off the string.

There are no gimmicks. This is the author's adaptation of a principle developed by Jack Miller and Peter Warlock.

METHOD: Use a 40″ shoelace or piece of string. Knot the ends. Place the string in your pocket until ready to perform the routine. Also required is an opaque 18″ handkerchief. A linen table napkin can also be used.

Remove the string from the pocket. Hold it as shown in Figure 39. Borrow a finger ring or plastic bracelet. Display the ring as shown in Figure 39.

Place the ring on the table. Then pick up the handkerchief and use it to cover the string as the string is placed on the table. Let the ends of the string protrude from the left side of the handkerchief as in Figure 38.

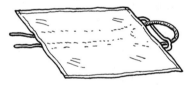

**Fig. 38**

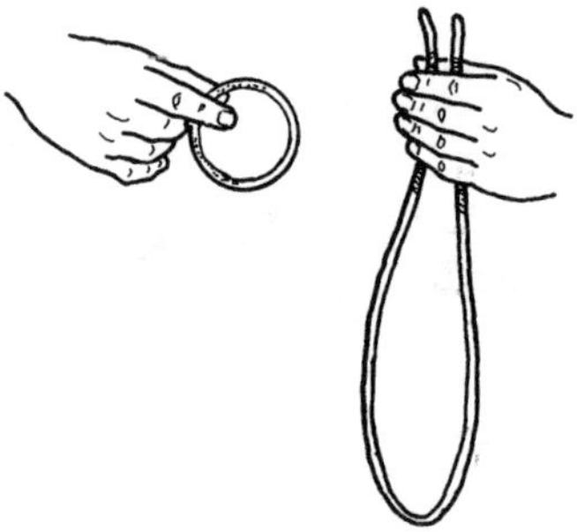

**Fig. 39**

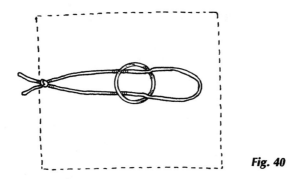

**Fig. 40**

Place the ring under the handkerchief. When it is out of sight, slide it over the string to about the center, Figure 40. In Figure 40 the handkerchief is shown by dotted lines.

Bring the center of the string down, Figure 41. Place the left first finger at point A and the left thumb at point B in Figure 41. Draw or pinch this portion of the string together, Figure 42. Note in Figure 42 that the left second, third and fourth fingers touch the upper strand of string. This is to keep the strand stationary for the next move.

Place the right first finger at point C and the right thumb at point D, as shown in Figure 42. The right hand then moves the string as indicated in Figure 43.

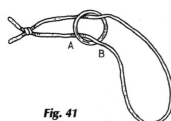

**Fig. 41**

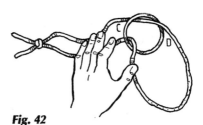

**Fig. 42**

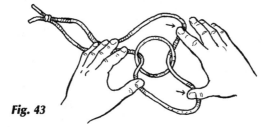

**Fig. 43**

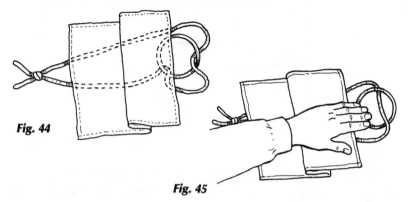

Fig. 44

Fig. 45

Remove the hands from under the handkerchief. Then draw back the handkerchief to reveal that the ring is apparently linked onto the string, Figure 38. An exposed view is given in Figure 44.

At this point you can strengthen the illusion by pushing the ring forward with the left hand, Figure 45. The back of the left hand conceals the true situation from audience view. Keep the left hand in place as the left thumb and first finger grasp the handkerchief, Figure 46, and draw the handkerchief over the ring so the ring is completely covered. Grasp the ends of the string and slowly draw the string out, Figure 47.

The ring has somehow come free of the string. All that remains is to lift the handkerchief and return the ring to its owner.

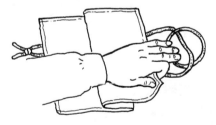

Fig. 46

Fig. 47

## 6.  No Pockets

Slydini invented a sight gag that produces an amusing visual illusion. The only requirement is that the magician must be wearing a shirt or jacket that has no pockets. Needing a handkerchief for a trick, the magician looks about, then pats the nonexistent pocket and proceeds to remove a handkerchief from it. He performs the trick, then returns the handkerchief to the nonexistent pocket.

There is no patter. It is purely an interlude. Some in the audience will catch it and wonder if they can believe what they saw. No attention is called to it, and the gag is over in a second.

METHOD: Use a handkerchief that will fit comfortably in the hand. A 12″ silk handkerchief might be best to practice with. You are seated at a table with the handkerchief in the right trouser pocket.

While talking with others at the table, reach into the pocket, gather the handkerchief in a loose fist, remove it and place in on the lap. Do not call attention to this. Make it appear as if you are searching in the pocket for loose change or some other object.

When ready to perform, drop both hands into the lap. The right hand gathers the handkerchief and holds it in the loosely curled fingers. Glance toward the left side of the jacket to a point where the handkerchief pocket would be. Your left hand reaches up almost in an absentminded gesture, to the level of the nonexistent pocket. Then allow the left hand to drop to the lap.

Now bring both hands up to the nonexistent pocket. The left hand fakes the action of opening the pocket by having the left thumb pantomime the action of pulling open the top of the pocket. The right hand then pats the nonexistent pocket. All of this time, the right fingers are curled inward to hold the concealed handkerchief in place.

The right hand now remains stationary as the left hand removes the handkerchief, Figure 48. Not a word is said. You now go ahead with the trick that requires the handkerchief. If you had no trick in mind, the handkerchief can be used to pat the forehead.

For the finish, the handkerchief is made to vanish by a reversal of the above moves. The handkerchief is in the right hand. Both hands go to the right side of the jacket to the location of a nonexistent pocket on the right side.

The left hand, palm toward the body, contacts the jacket at the point where a handkerchief pocket would be. The left thumb pretends to open the pocket.

The right hand then tucks the handkerchief into the nonexistent pocket. The handkerchief really goes into the slightly curled fingers of the left hand, Figure 49.

The right hand, having completed its task, drops down to the level of the waist. The left hand remains stationary. Then the right hand moves up and pokes the handkerchief a bit farther down into the pocket.

Finally, both hands drop to the lap. Allow the left hand to release the handkerchief. Proceed from here with your next trick.

The best way to get an authentic look to the handling is to sit before a mirror and go through the actual motions of removing a handkerchief from the pocket. Emulate these actions when you perform "No Pockets."

## 7. Crazy Compass

The magician tells the story of how Columbus discovered America with a compass that acted with a mind of its own. All ends well with the production of an American flag from the compass.

METHOD: The cardboard compass was invented by Terri Rogers. To see how it works, fold a sheet of paper into fourths as shown by the dotted lines in Figure 50. Then construct a tube by folding the sides over and holding the shape in place with transparent tape, Figure 51.

Fold the tube flat. Then form a nose and tail by cutting along the dotted lines shown in Figure 52. Hold the apparatus as shown in Figure 53. Remark that this is the compass used by Columbus. It pointed west, indicating that he should travel in that direction to find India.

After traveling for weeks and finding nothing, he thought it best to change direction. Grasp the nose of the compass with the right hand, Figure 54. Turn the compass around end for end. Press the apparatus in the direction of the arrows in Figure 55.

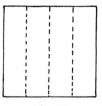

**Fig. 50**

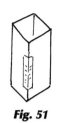

**Fig. 51**

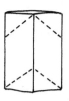

**Fig. 52**

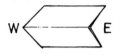

W ←—————→ E

**Fig. 53**

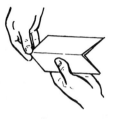

**Fig. 54**

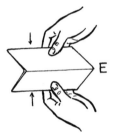

E

**Fig. 55**

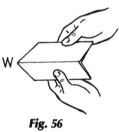

W ←

**Fig. 56**

FLAP

POCKET →

**Fig. 57**

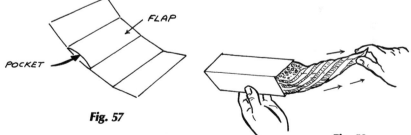

**Fig. 58**

The tube will open and fold flat the other way, producing a compass arrow that has instantly changed direction and again points west, Figure 56.

Grasp the nose of the compass again, Figure 54. Turn the compass around end for end so it points east. Then press on the apparatus, Figure 55, to make it change direction, Figure 56.

Remark that the compass insisted Columbus head west. He did, with the well-known result. Here you produce the American flag.

The production of the flag depends on another bit of preparation. The tube should be made of cardboard. Glue or tape a flap to one panel of the tube, Figure 57. The flap should be of the same material as the tube itself so it blends in well. The flag is then poked into the compartment indicated by the arrow in Figure 57.

Bring the sides of the tube together and tape them as in Figure 51. Then form the nose and tail, Figure 52. Perform the trick as described above. After you have demonstrated a few times that the compass arrow insists in pointing west, produce the flag, Figure 58.

The tube can also be used in another presentation as a rocket that goes up into space, then magically changes direction when it has to land on a distant planet.

# THE CORDS OF PHANTASIA

## 8. The Cords of Phantasia

Ottokar Fisher's famous trick, "The Cords of Phantasia," is one of those rare effects that work equally well as a stage trick or a close-up trick. As seen by the audience, several handkerchiefs are knotted onto two lengths of rope. The ropes themselves are then tied around the handkerchiefs. Instantly and visibly, the handkerchiefs free themselves from the ropes.

There are no gimmicks, no preparation and no secret moves. Everything may be examined before and after the trick.

METHOD: Required are two 6' lengths of rope and two 18" handkerchiefs. You will also need a magic wand or some similarly shaped article.

Drape the ropes over the wand. Have a spectator from the audience hold the ends of the wand. Grasp the ropes as shown in Figure 59 and tie a simple overhand knot, Figure 60. As you do this, remark that a magician and his assistant agreed to accept a challenge: They would be securely tied with rope and would have 30 seconds in which to free themselves. The magician knew he could do it because his magic wand had the power to free him from any restraint.

21

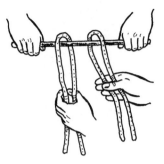

*Fig. 59*

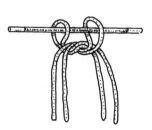

*Fig. 60*

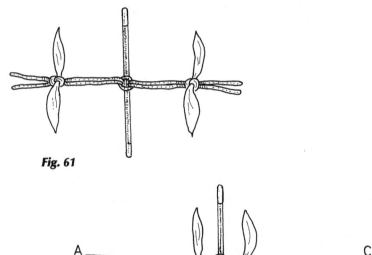

*Fig. 61*

*Fig. 62*

Remark that you will let the two handkerchiefs represent the magician and his assistant. Tie one on either side of the wand, Figure 61. The handkerchiefs are fastened to the ropes with simple overhand knots.

After the handkerchiefs have been tied to the ropes, move them in close to the wand, Figure 62.

Grasp either end A or end B with the left hand, and end C or end D with the right hand. It makes no difference which ends you choose, as long as you grasp one from each side. Tie an overhand knot with these ends, Figure 63. Pull the knot snug. Have the spectators grasp the ends of the rope, Figure 64.

Say, "Even though it looked impossible, the magician knew he and his assistant could escape because of the power of the wand. Just then someone noticed the wand and took it away."

As you say this, slide the wand out and hold it in the right hand. "The situation might have been hopeless, but the wand had already done its work."

Have the spectators pull sharply on the ends of the rope. At the same time, grasp the handkerchiefs and pull them downward. The result is that the handkerchiefs seemingly melt off the ropes, Figure 65. If the spectators pull sharply enough, the handkerchiefs will jump off the ropes of their own accord. By grasping the handkerchiefs and pulling them away from the ropes, you insure that the penetration is accomplished.

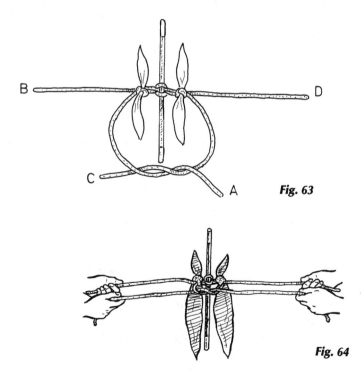

B                                                    D

C

A        *Fig. 63*

*Fig. 64*

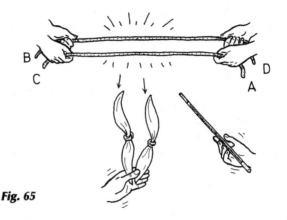

***Fig. 65***

As to why the trick works, note in Figure 60 that, if the wand were removed and the ends of the ropes pulled in opposite directions, the knot would dissolve, leaving you with a rope in each hand. To disguise this simple secret, one end of each rope is knotted in Figure 63. In a subtle way you have switched one end of each rope. When the wand is removed and the ends of the ropes pulled, the knot will dissolve. This allows the handkerchiefs to slide free from the ropes.

## 9. The Antique Shop

The magician patters that, while looking through an antique shop, his eye was caught by a box in one corner. The owner of the shop said the box and its contents once belonged to an escape artist. Inside the box were two ropes and a handkerchief. The magician tied the ropes around the handkerchief, then threaded the ropes through holes in the box and tied the ropes in a knot.

The escape artist's props must have remembered how to free themselves, because instantly the ropes penetrated the handkerchief and the box. All can be left with the audience for examination.

METHOD: Required is a cardboard box measuring about 10″ square and about 5″ in depth. These dimensions are not crucial. You may find a larger or smaller box just as suitable.

The box has holes in the sides through which two ropes will be threaded. Also required are two ropes, each about 5′ long, and an 18″ handkerchief.

The trick is based on "The Cords of Phantasia" principle. The use of a box is the clever idea of Hans van Baaren. Begin by draping the ropes over the handkerchief, Figure 66. As in "The Cords of Phantasia," take the two ends of one rope in one hand and the two ends of the other rope in the other hand. Tie a single overhand knot, Figure 67.

Lower the ends of the ropes into the box, Figure 68. Thread the ends of one rope through the hole in one side of the box. Then thread the ends of the other rope through the hole in the other side of the box. A spectator can do this while you hold the handkerchief. The situation is shown in Figure 69.

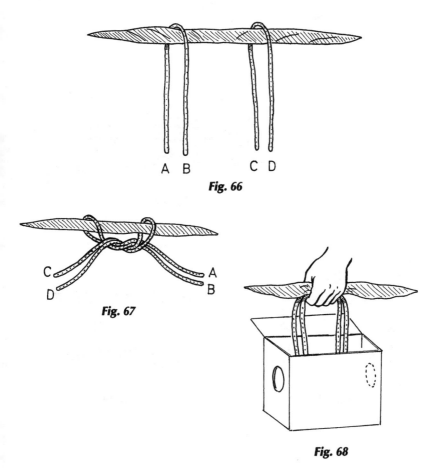

A  B        C  D

**Fig. 66**

C
D

A
B

**Fig. 67**

**Fig. 68**

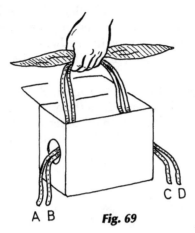

A B          *Fig. 69*

C D

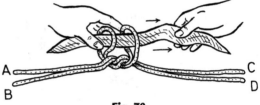

A                                    C

B                                    D

*Fig. 70*

*Fig. 71*

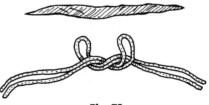

*Fig. 72*

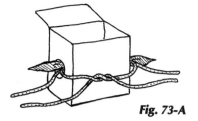

**Fig. 73-A**

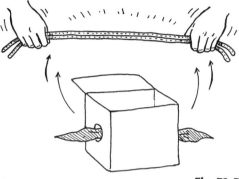

**Fig. 73-B**

Now lower the handkerchief into the box to thread the ends through the holes in the box. When the hands are out of sight inside the box, grasp the right end of the handkerchief with the right hand. The left hand slides the ropes almost to the left end of the handkerchief, Figure 70. The hands then thread the right end of the handkerchief through the hole in the right side of the box. The movement of the left hand should be smooth and unhurried.

You are now going to thread the left end of the handkerchief through the hole on the left side of the box. As you do, free the left end of the handkerchief completely from the ropes, then thread it through the hole in the left side of the box.

Figure 71 shows the apparatus as it appears to the audience. Figure 72 shows an exposed view with the box removed to demonstrate the actual situation; the handkerchief is free of the ropes.

Take one of the rope ends from the left side of the box and tie it to a rope end from the right side of the box, Figure 73-A. Grasp the left ends of the ropes with the left hand, the right ends with the right hand.

Pull upward and the ropes will come free of the handkerchief and the box, Figure 73-B. The patter is to the effect that the escape artist's apparatus still worked its magic.

## 10.  Ribbonesque

One of the classics in handkerchief magic is a trick known as "The Grandmother's Necklace." Based on a principle related to "The Cords of Phantasia," it is a trick in which three beads are threaded onto two ribbons or cords. The beads then mysteriously penetrate the cords. Edmund Younger, Eddie Joseph and others have expanded this close-up trick to stage proportions.

In the stage version, two ribbons are tied around an assistant's waist, Figure 74. A handkerchief is also tied to the ropes. In plain view of the audience, the assistant walks through the ribbons, Figure 75. It is an excellent, visually dramatic trick for platform or stage.

METHOD: Use two 9′ ribbons or ropes. Colorful ribbons can be bought in stores that sell sewing supplies. If ropes are used, make sure they are untreated cotton ropes, as cotton is easier to handle than treated or plastic-coated rope.

Beforehand, tie a loop of thread around the ribbons as shown in Figure 76. Use thread that is the same color as the ribbons so it will blend in. Cotton thread is preferred because it breaks more easily than thread made from synthetics.

**Fig. 74**

**Fig. 75**

When presenting the trick, display the ropes as shown in the exposed view of Figure 77. In actual handling the right fingers would be closed to conceal the preparation. Figure 77-A.

Pick up a handkerchief with the left hand. Allow the handkerchief to drape over the hand as indicated in Figure 78.

Place the ropes on top of the handkerchief, Figure 79. Then grasp end A of the handkerchief with the right hand, thumb below and fingers above, as shown in Figure 79.

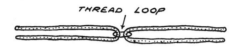

THREAD LOOP

**Fig. 76**

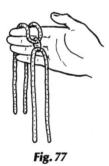

**Fig. 77**

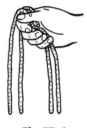

**Fig. 77-A**

A  B

**Fig. 78**

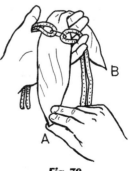

B

A

**Fig. 79**

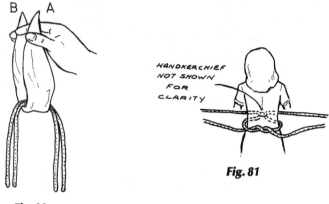

Fig. 81

Fig. 80

Bring end A up to meet end B. Grasp end B between the right first and second fingers, Figure 80. The ropes are now draped over the center of the handkerchief. Lift the handkerchief away from the left hand and display the apparatus for a second.

Tie a knot in the handkerchief. As you do, ask for the assistance of two men and one woman from the audience. Have one man grasp the ends of the ribbons on the left and the other man grasp the ends of the ribbons on the right. The men stand so the ribbons are loosely stretched between them.

Have the lady stand behind the ribbons. Take one end of a ribbon from each man. Tie the ends in an overhand knot behind the lady, Figure 81. Then hand the ribbons back; each man gets an end that previously belonged to the other man. Have the lady grasp the handkerchief. Then ask the men to pull the ribbons.

The thread loop breaks, allowing the lady to step forward, apparently right through the ribbons, as shown in Figure 75.

## 11.   Houdini's Coat

There are many ways "The Cords of Phantasia" principle can be exploited. The following is a presentation used by the author.

The magician mentions that a friend once gave him a jacket and a pair of handcuffs that belonged to Houdini. He threads two very large handkerchiefs or scarves through a pair of plastic handcuffs, Figure 82. (In Figures 82–85, the handkerchiefs are depicted ropelike for clarity in the method of tying.) The handkerchiefs are knotted around the cuffs, Figure 83. Then the ends of the handkerchiefs are threaded through Houdini's jacket, Figure 84. Two spectators are asked to hold the ends of the ropes.

The magician takes a handkerchief from each spectator and knots them with a single overhand knot, Figure 85. The ends are then given to the spectators to hold.

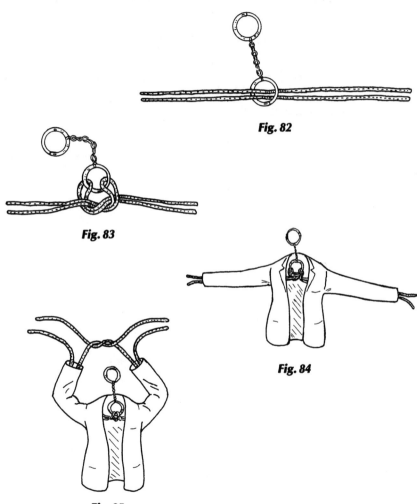

Fig. 82

Fig. 83

Fig. 84

Fig. 85

The magician reaches inside the jacket and releases the handcuffs. As he does, he says, "Houdini freed himself from the handcuffs." Then have the spectators pull sharply on the ends of the handkerchiefs. As this is done, the magician says, "And Houdini's jacket then freed itself from the handkerchiefs!" As this line is delivered, the jacket comes free of the handkerchiefs.

METHOD: The tying of the handkerchiefs is done exactly as described above. The only point that needs to be explained is the method of releasing the handcuffs.

Plastic handcuffs are available in toy stores. The key needed to unlock the cuffs is hidden under your wristwatch or in the inside pocket of the jacket.

After the handkerchiefs are tied and the apparatus is as shown in Figure 85, step behind the jacket, so that the jacket is between you and the audience. Bring the hands together and grasp the handcuffs. Then use the hidden key to open the cuffs.

Release the cuffs from the handkerchiefs then have the spectators pull the ends of the handkerchiefs to release the jacket from the handkerchiefs.

# SILK APPEAR

The production of a brightly colored silk handkerchief is one of the prettiest magical effects. Many magicians use silk productions as opening tricks because of their dramatic visual appeal. This chapter describes two folds that are basic to handkerchief magic. The folds are applied to some different and colorful production tricks. For best results, use silk handkerchiefs.

## 12. The Trap Fold

The trap fold allows you to roll a silk into a compact bundle that will open instantly when produced.

Spread an 18" silk out flat on the table. Fold corner A in toward the center, Figure 86. Then fold corner B in toward the center, Figure 87. In a similar way, fold corners C and D in toward the center. The result at this point is shown in Figure 88.

The process is now repeated. Fold corner E in toward the center, Figure 89. Similarly, fold corners F, G and H in toward the center. Continue folding the corners in toward the center until the bundle is small enough for the trick in question. Generally it is enough to reduce the bundle to a size about 2" in diameter, Figure 90.

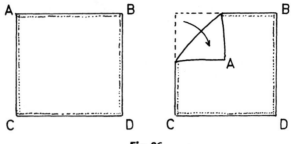

*Fig. 86*

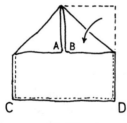

*Fig. 87*

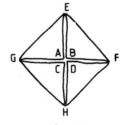

*Fig. 88*

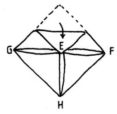

*Fig. 89*

*Fig. 90*

The trap-folded silk in not freestanding. It must be held together with a paper clip, rubber band or other object to keep it from unfolding. The trap-folded silk has the advantage that, once released, it quickly expands.

The trap fold can be used to produce a silk in a surprising manner. Trap fold a silk as described. Tuck the silk into the bend of the elbow, Figure 90-A. If the arm is kept bent at the elbow, the silk will not be seen by the audience.

The trick is done as an opening trick. With the trap-folded silk concealed as in Figure 90-A, face the audience. Wiggle the fingers of both hands to emphasize that both hands are empty. Then look upward. Reach into the air with both hands in a quick motion. Straighten the arms as you do so. The quick action of the arms will propel the silk into the air, Figure 90-B. Catch the silk and display it to the audience.

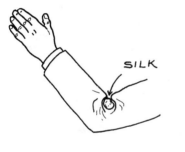

SILK

**Fig. 90-A**                **Fig. 90-B**

## 13. The Birthday

The magician remarks that he was on the way home when he realized it was his wife's birthday and he had not bought her a present. He solved the problem by rolling up that day's newspaper into two tubes and producing a colorful scarf from each!

METHOD: Use about ten sheets of tabloid-size newspaper to form the tubes. Cut the sheets in half, Figure 91, and roll up each set of half sheets to form tubes measuring about 11½" in height and 3" in diameter. The tubes are held secure by tape, staples or paper clips, Figure 92.

CUT IN HALF

10 SHEETS

**Fig. 91**

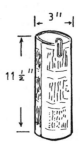

**Fig. 92**

SILKS

**Fig. 93**

FINGERS COVER SILKS

**Fig. 94**

**Fig. 95**

Trap-fold two 18″ silks. Each silk bundle is held securely near the top of a tube with a paper clip, Figure 93. The tubes thus prepared are on the table until you are ready to perform. Near each tube is an ordinary drinking glass.

Remark that you forgot your wife's birthday. Quickly you looked through that day's newspaper and discovered that silk scarves were on sale. You made two tubes from the newspaper. As you speak, grasp each tube as shown in Figure 94. The hand reaches inside the tube and covers the silk. Lift each tube and hold it so the audience can see inside. Because each hand covers a silk, each tube appears empty.

Set each tube down over a glass. As you do, push the silks downward until the silks are free of the paper clips. The silks will then fall into the glasses, opening as they fall.

Remark that your wife just walked into the room at that moment. She was about to ask if you had forgotten something, but before she had a chance to speak, her present materialized. Lift one tube to reveal a silk inside the glass, Figure 95. Then lift the other tube to reveal another handkerchief.

You may find that one silk will not open out fully before it hits the glass. If this happens, pick up a pair of scissors and say that you used the scissors as a magic wand. Poke the scissors down into the tube, poking the silk into the glass. Then lift the glass to show the silk.

## 14.  The Coil Fold

There are several methods of folding silks so that they take up little space, allowing them to be concealed from audience view. These folds keep the silk in a secure bundle that will not open accidentally, yet the silk will snap open when required.

The coil fold is one of the best such folds. It works as follows. Spread an 18″ silk out flat, as shown in Figure 96. Fold corners B and D in toward the center, Figure 97. Fold E-F and G-H in toward the center, Figure 98. Continue folding the sides in toward the center until the bundle is about 3″ wide.

Fold the left half over onto the right half, Figure 99. Fold about 2″ of end A over at right angles to the silk, Figure 100. Starting at end A, roll the strip down toward end C, Figure 101. Roll the silk as tightly as possible.

When the rolling is complete, tuck end C into a fold in the bundle as shown in Figure 102. Another method is to tuck end C into the end opposite end A as indicated in Figure 103. Use the blunt end of a toothpick to tuck in end C.

The silk bundle can be moved about without fear it will open. To cause the silk to open, grasp end A and snap the silk. The silk will open out to its full length instantly, Figure 104.

An application to an opening trick is as follows. Coil fold a red silk and tuck it into the right jacket sleeve. Coil fold a yellow silk and tuck it into the left jacket sleeve. When the preparation is complete, keep the arms at waist level so the silks will not fall from the sleeves.

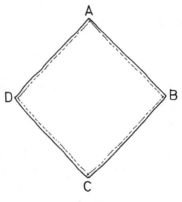

**Fig. 96**

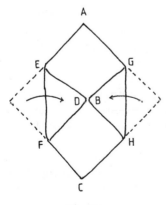

**Fig. 97**

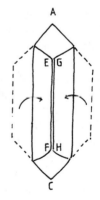

**Fig. 98**

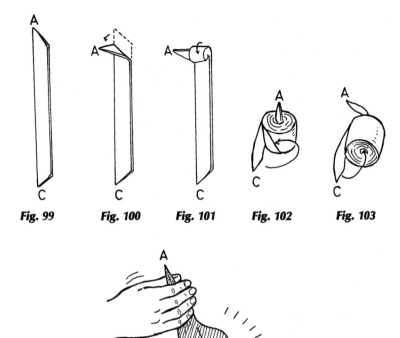

Fig. 99      Fig. 100      Fig. 101      Fig. 102      Fig. 103

Fig. 104

Have a paper bag handy. Ask a spectator to check that the bag is empty. Reach into the bag with the right hand, allowing the red silk to fall from the sleeve into the bag. Bring the right hand out empty. Reach into the bag with the left hand, allowing the yellow silk to fall from the sleeve into the bag. Bring the left hand out empty.

Say, "I thought I had put a couple of invisible handkerchiefs in here." Reach in again with the right hand. Grasp one of the silks by the protruding corner, bring the hand out of the bag and snap the silk so it releases to its full length.

Reach in with the left hand, grasp the other silk by the protruding corner, bring the silk out of the bag and snap the corner so the silk releases to its full length.

## 15.    A Novel Production

A handkerchief is borrowed and draped over the right hand. The left hand reaches under the handkerchief and produces a wand. The wand is waved over the handkerchief. Then the magician reaches under the handkerchief and produces a colorful silk. This trick can be done at any time in the performance.

METHOD: An 18″ red silk is prepared with the coil fold, but when you reach Figure 100, place a 7″ wand or pen on the silk as shown in Figure 105. Complete the coil fold. The prepared silk will look as it does in Figure 106. Place the prepared silk in the inside left jacket pocket. Put a white cotton handkerchief in the same pocket.

**Fig. 105**

**Fig. 106**

When you are ready to perform, show your hands empty. Reach into the inside right jacket pocket with the left hand as though getting the handkerchief. Remove the left hand. Then reach into the left inside jacket pocket with the right hand. Remove the coiled silk and pen from the pocket and drop them down the left sleeve. The left arm is bent at the elbow, Figure 107, to keep the apparatus in place.

Remove the cotton handkerchief and show both sides. Then hold it in the right hand. As you display the handkerchief once more, drop the left arm to the side. The coiled silk and pen will drop down the sleeve into the left hand, Figure 108.

Bring the left hand up behind the cotton handkerchief, Figure 109. Drape the handkerchief over the left hand, then grasp the concealed apparatus with the right hand as you bring the right hand away from the left, Figure 110.

Reach under the handkerchief with the left hand and slide the pen out from the coiled red silk. Produce the pen by bringing it out into view as shown in Figure 111. The silk is concealed under the handkerchief.

Wave the pen over the handkerchief. Then place the pen into the handkerchief pocket of the jacket. Turn the right hand palm up. Reach into the folds of the handkerchief and produce the red silk, Figure 112.

Some white cotton handkerchiefs are translucent and may not be able to conceal the bright color of the silk. If you find this to be the case, make sure the red silk is completely concealed by the right hand when you reach the point shown in Figure 111.

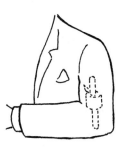

**Fig. 107**

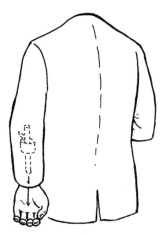

**Fig. 108**

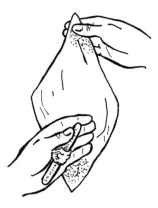

**Fig. 109**

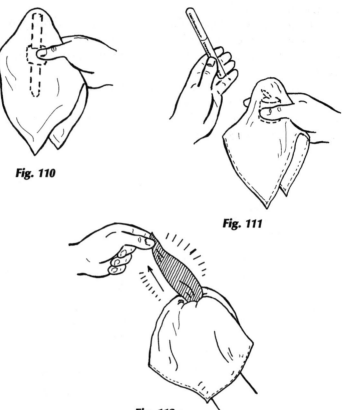

Fig. 110

Fig. 111

Fig. 112

## 16.   Silk from Silk

The magician borrows a handkerchief from a spectator in the audience. Announcing that handkerchiefs have a thread woven into the cloth that can be made into another handkerchief, the magician finds the thread, pulls it upward, and it blossoms into another handkerchief!

METHOD: Because of the manner in which the trick is prepared, "Silk from Silk" should be done as an opening trick. Have a white silk rolled in a coil fold. Tuck it into the jacket at the bend of the elbow, Figure 113. Keep the arm slightly bent so the silk will be concealed from audience view.

Borrow a white handkerchief and put it in the right hand. If one is not available, you can have a white cotton handkerchief in the right jacket pocket. Remove it, let a spectator unfold it and verify that it is unprepared, then take it back.

Drape the handkerchief over the left arm at the elbow, just over the concealed silk, Figure 114. Show the hands empty. Then grasp the handkerchief with the right hand. The right thumb goes under the handkerchief and contacts the concealed silk, Figure 115. The silk is brought out concealed behind the handkerchief, Figure 116.

COIL - FOLDED SILK

**Fig. 113**

**Fig. 114**

**Fig. 115**

**Fig. 116**

Explain that all handkerchiefs have an extra thread that can be woven into a silk. As you speak, pretend to search for the thread. Pull the invisible thread upward, then pull the end of the concealed silk upward, Figure 117.

The silk will unfurl as it is pulled. Finish by displaying the silk with the left hand. Toss the cotton handkerchief back to the spectator.

**Fig. 117**

## 17. Collared

If you have just performed "Silk from Silk," this trick is a good follow-up. Showing his hands unmistakably empty, the magician produces a handkerchief from within the folds of a borrowed handkerchief.

METHOD: Have a silk rolled with the coil-fold. Tuck it under the jacket collar between the jacket and the shirt, Figure 118.

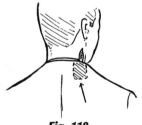

**Fig. 118**

Borrow a handkerchief. Show the hands empty. Then remark that static electricity can be used to weave a silk. Bring the left hand up to a point near your left ear. Rub the borrowed handkerchief against the left elbow, Figure 119.

Transfer the handkerchief to the left hand. Then bring the right hand up so that the fingers contact the hidden silk. Rub the handkerchief against the right elbow, Figure 120. Grasp the concealed silk with the right thumb and fingers, Figure 121. Close the hand over the silk so the silk is concealed in the right palm. Raise the right hand so it is almost at eye level.

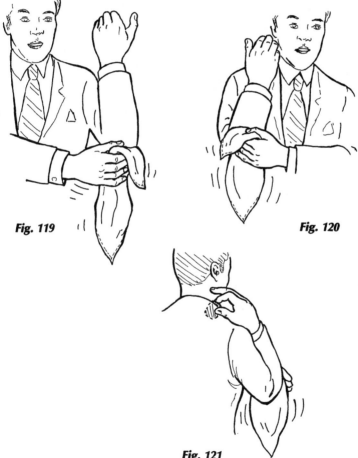

**Fig. 119**

**Fig. 120**

**Fig. 121**

Bring the right hand up in back of the handkerchief held by the left hand. The handkerchief provides cover for the silk concealed in the right palm, Figure 122.

Clip the coiled silk behind the handkerchief as shown in Figure 123. This allows the left hand to tug on the handkerchief, as if to make an imaginary adjustment. The left hand then grasps the top corner of the coiled silk and pulls upward to produce the silk.

*Fig. 122*                              *Fig. 123*

# PENETRATIONS

A popular trick with handkerchiefs is the effect where one or more objects penetrate a handkerchief. This chapter will describe the best-known method and several offbeat approaches to the penetration effect. This type of trick works especially well with a borrowed handkerchief. Convinced that you have torn a hole in his handkerchief to bring about the penetration, the spectator will be surprised (and no doubt relieved) when the handkerchief is returned to him unharmed.

## 18. Freefall

The magician borrows a handkerchief and a pen. He drapes the handkerchief over his hand. He remarks that, according to theory, handkerchiefs are woven in such a way that small holes will repair themselves. Offering to test the theory with the other fellow's handkerchief, he pokes the pen straight down through the center of the handkerchief.

Amazingly, no damage has been done to the handkerchief.

METHOD: Place the tip of the left thumb and first finger together, Figure 124, to form a circle. Drape the borrowed handkerchief over the left hand. Poke a hole in the center of the handkerchief with the

*Fig. 124*

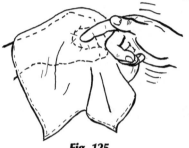

*Fig. 125*

*Fig. 126*

*Fig. 127*

*Fig. 128*

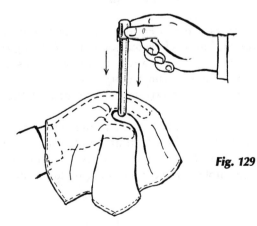

*Fig. 129*

right first finger, Figure 125. As you make the hole deeper, the right second finger pushes a section of cloth into the hole, Figure 126. This creates a trough in the handkerchief. Note that the left thumb and first finger are separated as the trough is formed. This allows the section of cloth to be pushed between these fingers, as in Figure 126.

To conceal this action from audience view, poke the hole as shown in Figure 127 with a quick motion repeated two or three times. Each time the hole is made deeper by the first finger. When it reaches the position of Figure 128 and is almost hidden from audience view, the right second finger forms the trough.

Place the pen into the hole as shown in Figure 129. Hold it in place with the left thumb and first finger. The palm-down right hand then taps against the top of the pen. Do not release the left hand's grip on the pen. Make it appear as if the handkerchief is offering resistance to the pen. Pretend to increase the force exerted by the right hand. Remark to the undoubtedly worried spectator that you are practically certain the handkerchief will repair itself after the center has been torn by the pen.

Ease pressure on the pen, allowing it to sink down into the trough each time it is tapped. At about the halfway point, the pen will look as shown in Figure 130. Tap it again, this time letting it fall through, as shown by the arrows in Figure 130.

Then spread the handkerchief and return it unharmed to the spectator.

If you are seated at a table, you can make the pen vanish. Loosen the cap on the pen. Then pretend to tap the pen through the handkerchief, as in Figure 130. When just the cap is visible at the top of the handkerchief, pretend to be having trouble. Say, "I'll just tear the handkerchief a bit more to get the pen through." As you speak, lower the hand so the bottom of the handkerchief is just below the level of the table top. Reach under the handkerchief with the right hand and pull the pen free, Figure 131.

Drop the pen into the lap. The pen can also be dropped into the jacket sleeve. Make believe you are having trouble finding the pen. Pull the cap upward with the right hand. Then toss the handkerchief to the table to show that the pen has somehow vanished.

Although this method of forming a trough is one of the most popular, some people may find it difficult to cover the action. Other methods in this chapter rely on different handlings and different approaches to bring about the desired effect.

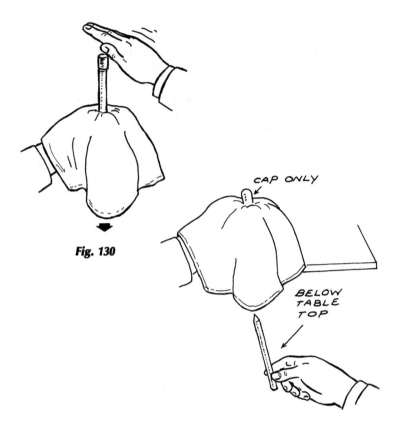

Fig. 130

CAP ONLY

BELOW
TABLE
TOP

Fig. 131

## 19.  Half Thru

Seated at a table, the magician makes a pen penetrate a borrowed handkerchief, but in the process, the pen gets stuck halfway through. The handkerchief is shown on both sides. The pen is unmistakably partway through, yet at the finish the handkerchief is seen to be unharmed.

METHOD: This is a different way to form the trough in the handkerchief. Fold a handkerchief in half. Hold the handkerchief in the right hand so the center is draped over the fingers, Figure 132.

Bring the handkerchief over to the left hand to a position between the left thumb and first finger, Figure 133. In a continuing action, flip

the top of the handkerchief over the left hand in the direction of the
arrow shown in Figure 133.

The result is that a trough or channel has automatically been
formed in the handkerchief as shown in Figure 134. To make sure the
trough cannot be seen, keep the back of the left hand toward the
audience. Also, keep the left thumb below the level of the left first
finger.

Loosen the cap of the pen. Place the pen in the trough as shown in
Figure 134. The hand is positioned near the table top so that the
handkerchief hangs just below the level of the table top.

**Fig. 132**

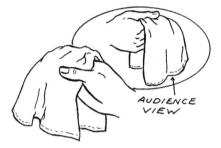

AUDIENCE VIEW

**Fig. 133**

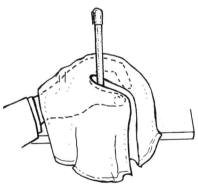

**Fig. 134**

Using the palm of the right hand, push the pen downward. Pretend to use great force to accomplish this, as if you are forcing the pen to tear through the center of the handkerchief.

When the pen has been pushed down about halfway, pretend to have trouble. Reach under the handkerchief and grasp the pen, Figure 135.

Pull the pen free of the cap. The left thumb and first finger hold the cap in place. The right hand pulls the pen down and out of the trough, then up and under the handkerchief. This action is covered by the fact that it occurs below the level of the table top.

Push the top of the pen into the cap. This must be done through the thickness of the handkerchief. With the pen jammed into the cap, the situation is as shown in Figure 136.

Tell the audience that the pen got stuck halfway through the handkerchief. Display the handkerchief on both sides as shown in Figure 136. It appears as if the pen protrudes partway through the handkerchief.

Gather up the handkerchief. Pull the cap free, then allow the pen to fall to the table. Apologize for damaging the handkerchief and toss it back to its owner.

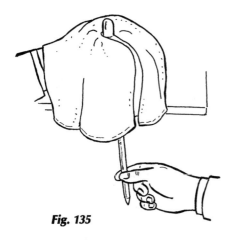

**Fig. 135**

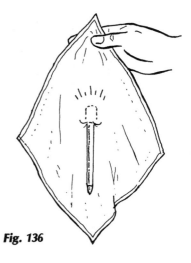

**Fig. 136**

## 20.  Exit Coin

A coin penetrates down through a handkerchief and then back up again. There is no secret trough formed in the handkerchief. The coin may be marked.

METHOD: Two identical coins are used. Half dollars are large American coins that give maximum visibility, but American quarters, British 50-pence pieces or other coins will work as well.

Have a half dollar in the left jacket pocket along with the handkerchief. The duplicate half dollar is in the right jacket pocket. This is the only preparation.

To perform the routine, place both hands in the pockets. The left hand grasps the half dollar and holds it with the second and third fingers. The handkerchief is grasped between the thumb and first finger. As the left hand comes out of the pocket, it looks like Figure 137. The coin is hidden by the handkerchief.

The right hand removes the other half dollar from the right jacket pocket. The coin is placed on the table while the right hand adjusts the handkerchief so it covers the left hand. The right hand then places its coin in the center of the handkerchief, directly over the concealed coin, Figure 138.

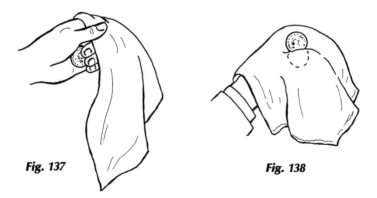

**Fig. 137**                    **Fig. 138**

The right hand reaches under the handkerchief and grasps both coins as indicated in Figure 139. The upper coin is outside the handkerchief and must be grasped through the cloth.

The right hand moves up and down, then up again, and then down again. On the final downward movement, the visible coin is pulled down and out of sight as shown in Figure 140. Without hesitation, the right hand pulls the duplicate coin out from under the handkerchief and displays it as shown in Figure 141. It appears as if the coin has penetrated the handkerchief.

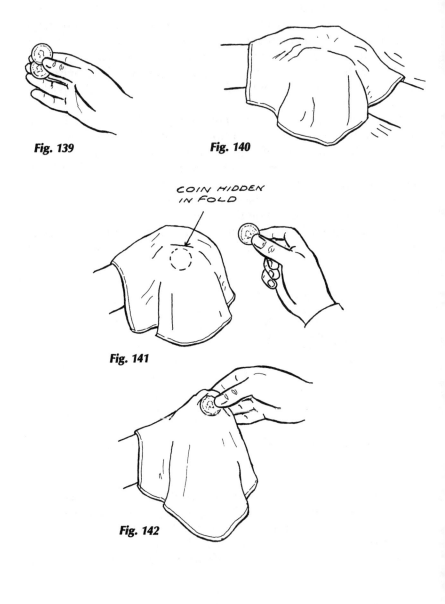

**Fig. 139**

**Fig. 140**

COIN HIDDEN IN FOLD

**Fig. 141**

**Fig. 142**

The coin is placed under the handkerchief. As soon as it is out of sight, the right hand gets rid of the coin by dropping it into the left jacket sleeve. If you wear a watch, the duplicate coin can be slipped under the watch.

Bring the right hand out, grasp the coin and bring it up behind the handkerchief, Figure 142. It appears as if the coin is under the handkerchief. Pull the coin up with a sharp upward motion of your right hand. Toss the coin out onto the table. Then return the handkerchief to the spectator.

## 21.   General Rise

This is a utility method of causing an object to penetrate a handkerchief. The object can be a pen, pencil, comb, spoon or any similar object—even a toothbrush. It can be a coin or ring, a playing card, a 6″ ruler or a lollipop. You do not form a trough in the handkerchief. The borrowed object is the one that penetrates the handkerchief.

METHOD: Use any opaque handkerchief 18″ or larger. Drape it over your left hand as shown in Figure 143. Note that the front of the handkerchief hangs lower than the back. This means that corners C and D are lower than corners A and B. Your left thumb should be about even with the middle finger as indicated in Figure 144.

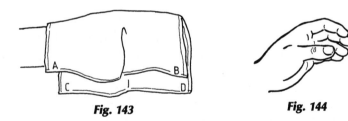

**Fig. 143**          **Fig. 144**

**Fig. 145**

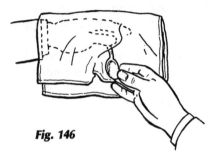

**Fig. 146**

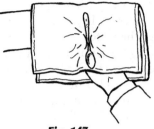

**Fig. 147**

**Fig. 148**

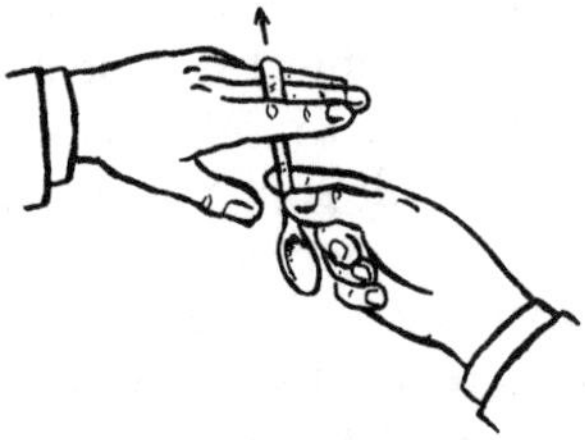

**Fig. 149**

Pick up an object such as a spoon with the right hand. Display it by holding it up behind the handkerchief, Figure 145. Then bring it down so it is behind the handkerchief, screened from audience view.

When the spoon is in this position, press the left thumb against the spoon, Figure 146. Since the thumb is under the handkerchief, it presses against the spoon through a thickness of cloth.

The right hand continues downward and then up under the handkerchief as if it held the spoon. When the right hand is under the handkerchief, it pinches the spoon through a thickness of cloth, Figure 147. Release the left thumb's grip on the spoon. The spoon is now held by the right thumb and first finger through the cloth.

The next maneuver creates the convincing illusion that the spoon is really under the handkerchief. The right hand pushes the spoon upward between the left first and second fingers to produce a bulge at the top of the handkerchief, Figure 148. An exposed view with the handkerchief removed is shown in Figure 149.

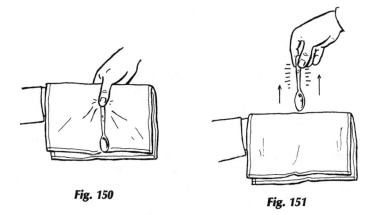

Fig. 150

Fig. 151

The right hand then brings the spoon back to the position of Figure 147. The right hand comes out from under the handkerchief and grasps the spoon as shown in Figure 150. Pull upward with the right thumb in a quick motion. The spoon apparently penetrates the handkerchief, Figure 151.

If you are seated at the dinner table, you can do the trick with a linen table napkin and a spoon from the place setting.

## 22.  Pentapencil

A borrowed handkerchief is stretched out flat and held by two spectators. A square of newspaper is placed over the center of the handkerchief. A borrowed pencil is made to penetrate the center of the handkerchief and the newspaper, Figure 152. Although the newspaper is torn in the process, the handkerchief is not harmed.

Fig. 152

This trick is based on a fine effect of Emil Jarrow and Walter Schwartz. It can be performed close up or, as Jarrow did it, from the stage. It leaves a strong impression on the audience.

METHOD: The handkerchief should be as large as possible. An opaque 27″ handkerchief or table napkin would be ideal. The pencil should be about 3″ long. A cigarette, penknife, rolled dollar bill or similar object can also be used. The folded square of newspaper should measure about 12″ on a side.

Ask two spectators to assist. They hold the handkerchief outstretched in a horizontal position as shown in Figure 152. If you are performing this routine on the platform or stage, have the spectators hold the handkerchief so the front corners slope downward slightly. With the handkerchief tipped down toward the audience, the spectators get a clear view of the effect. The slant of the handkerchief also helps to hide the method from spectators sitting in the front rows.

Hold the pencil in the right hand, the point downward. Hold the square of newspaper in the left hand. Display the pencil and newspaper. Hold the newspaper over the center of the handkerchief as in Figure 152.

Move the right hand with the pencil under the handkerchief to the center. Pretend to push the pencil up through the center of the handkerchief. Act puzzled that it is not working. Withdraw the right hand. At the same time draw the left hand back so that the newspaper is in the position shown in Figure 153.

Say, "The pencil should be point upward." Turn the pencil around so it is as shown in Figure 153. Then say, "That's why I would never try this with my own handkerchief."

As the right hand moves under the handkerchief, you make the crucial maneuver. Secretly clip the pencil between the left second and third fingers, Figure 154. The newspaper hides the action. The right hand does not hesitate as it continues to move under the handkerchief.

As the right hand reaches the center of the handkerchief, the left hand simultaneously moves over the top of the handkerchief to the middle. When both hands are at the center of the handkerchief, the right hand pinches the eraser end of the pencil through the fabric of the handkerchief, Figure 155.

Make sure the center of the paper is just above the point of the pencil. Place the paper down on top of the pencil, then press down on the paper with the left hand so the pencil can penetrate the paper, Figure 156.

Pull the pencil all the way up through the paper with the left hand. Say, "The tear in the handkerchief is hardly noticeable if you keep the handkerchief folded up in your pocket." Pause a second for dramatic effect, then remove the paper to show the handkerchief is unharmed.

**Fig. 153**

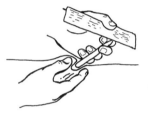

**Fig. 154**                    **Fig. 155**

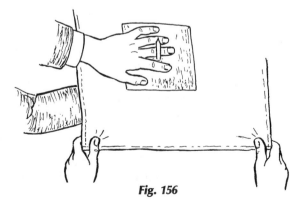

**Fig. 156**

## 23. Curio

Four coins are borrowed. The magician places them under the center of a handkerchief held outstretched by two spectators. The center of the handkerchief is covered with a square of paper. On command, any named coin penetrates the handkerchief.

This is the author's adaptation of Jarrow's "Pentapencil." Only the four coins are used. There are no extras, and the left hand is empty right up to the second the named coin penetrates the handkerchief.

METHOD: Use an opaque 27" handkerchief. As in the previous trick, it is held in a horizontal position by two spectators. The newspaper should measure about 14" square. Fold it in half and hold it with the thumb and little finger below, the other fingers on top, as shown in Figure 157. The paper is held so the center of the paper is over the near edge of the handkerchief.

***Fig. 157***

Hold a penny, nickel, dime and quarter in the right hand. Display the coins to the audience. Place the right hand under the handkerchief. Have the spectator name one coin. You can tell by touch which of the four coins is the coin named, or you can memorize which coin is in which position in the right hand.

Grasp that coin between the right thumb and first finger. The other three coins are held by the curled second, third and fourth fingers. Under cover of the handkerchief, toss or place the named coin in the left jacket sleeve as the right hand goes under the handkerchief, Figure 158.

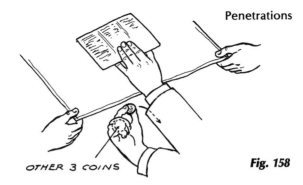

OTHER 3 COINS

**Fig. 158**

Bring the right hand under the handkerchief to a position at the center. At the same time, bring the left hand over the handkerchief to a position just above the center. As the left hand reaches the center of the handkerchief, allow the coin to slide out of the sleeve by tipping the left hand downward. The coin slides out under cover of the newspaper, Figure 159-A.

Grasp the coin through the handkerchief with the right hand. Place the newspaper down flat on the handkerchief so it still covers the coin. Then place the left hand down flat on the newspaper. Push the coin upward so it tears the paper. Withdraw it all the way with the left hand. Then bring the right hand into view, the hand open and palm up, to show the other three coins.

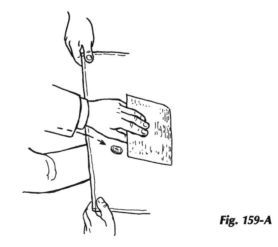

**Fig. 159-A**

The reader may wish to expolore other methods of accomplishing this effect: for example, say the right hand holds a coin and the left

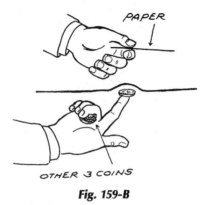

**Fig. 159-B**

hand a square of cardboard. The coin is balanced on the tip of the right first finger, Figure 159-B. The handkerchief is held outstretched by two spectators. The right hand starts to move under the handkerchief and the left hand over the handkerchief.

As soon as the right hand is out of sight, pinch the coin through the fabric by the left third and fourth fingers, Figure 159-C. The right hand moves under the handkerchief to a point near the middle. The left hand drops the coin onto the right arm as shown by the arrow in Figure 159-C.

Now the right arm moves back toward the body just enough for the coin to clear the handkerchief. The coin can then be pinched between the left third and fourth fingers, Figure 159-D.

Both hands move toward the center of the handkerchief, the left hand above and the right hand below the handkerchief. Drop the coin onto the handkerchief under the cardboard. Remove the cardboard to show that the coin has penetrated the handkerchief.

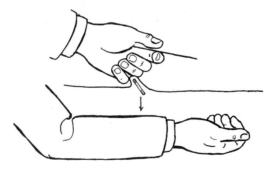

**Fig. 159-C**

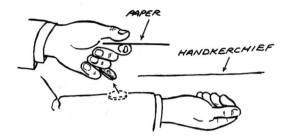

**Fig. 159-D**

## 24.  Pop Up

Sometimes a trick will generate interest because of the offbeat props the magician uses. Thimbles are not ordinarily employed in magic tricks, but this is a brilliant exception. As the audience sees it, a thimble penetrates a handkerchief. This trick, devised by Walter Schwartz, uses just one thimble and no gimmicks.

METHOD: Thimbles can be obtained from department stores and shops specializing in sewing goods. They are available in a variety of sizes. Also required is an opaque 18″ handkerchief.

Have the thimble on the right first finger. The handkerchief is held by an edge in the left hand. The thimble is displayed as shown in Figure 160.

**Fig. 160**

As the handkerchief covers the right hand, the right first finger curls inward and wedges the thimble in the crease of the thumb, Figure 161. The thimble is held in place by pressure of the thumb.

The first finger straightens as the handkerchief is draped over it, Figure 162. From the front, it appears as if the thimble has been placed under the center of the handkerchief. Make sure the thimble is not covered by the folds of the handkerchief.

Move the right hand up and down with a gentle motion. As you do, curl the first finger inward, Figure 163, so it enters the thimble through the thickness of the cloth. Straighten the forefinger to show the thimble now on the outside of the handkerchief, Figure 164.

When purchasing a thimble, find one that fits comfortably, then choose the next-largest size. This will allow the thimble to fit on the forefinger through a layer of cloth.

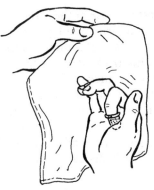

**Fig. 161**

**Fig. 162**

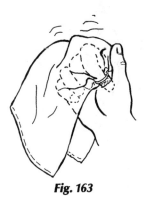

**Fig. 163**

**Fig. 164**

## 25.  Jump Up

This is Duke Stern's impromptu method of causing a pencil to penetrate a handkerchief.

Hold the pencil at about midpoint between the right thumb and first finger. Have the spectator grasp a handkerchief by the corners and cover the pencil. As the handkerchief is draped over the pencil, curl the right third and fourth fingers in front of the pencil, Figure 165.

You now seem to grasp the point of the pencil between the left thumb and first finger. Actually, the left hand grasps only the cloth. The right hand allows the pencil to swing down to a horizontal position. The pencil is clipped between the right second and third fingers, Figure 166.

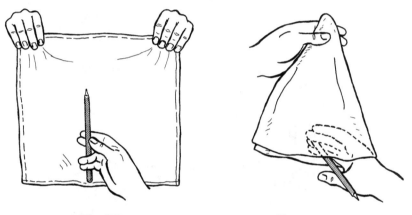

**Fig. 165**          **Fig. 166**

The right thumb, beneath the pencil, levers the pencil up to a vertical position outside the handkerchief, Figure 167. For maximum effectiveness, the action depicted in Figures 166 and 167 should be accomplished in a smooth, quick move. As soon as the pencil is upright, the point is gripped by the left thumb, Figure 167.

Curl the left fingers into a loose fist. This has the effect of wrapping the handkerchief around the pencil. Then tap the right palm against the base of the pencil, Figure 168, causing the pencil apparently to penetrate the handkerchief.

Fig. 167

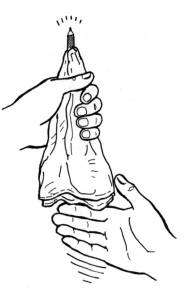

Fig. 168

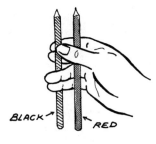

BLACK → ← RED

Fig. 169

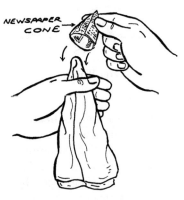

NEWSPAPER CONE →

Fig. 170

There is a clever variation on this effect. Get a black-lead pencil and a red-lead pencil. Hold both in the right hand, but hold the black pencil in the grip depicted in Figure 165. The red pencil is simply held between the right thumb and first finger. The position is indicated in Figure 169. Have the pencils covered with the handkerchief. Perform the move already described to get the black pencil outside the handkerchief. Then ask the spectator whether he prefers red or black. If he says black, make the black pencil penetrate the handkerchief.

If he says red, make the black pencil penetrate the handkerchief, remove the black pencil with the right hand and say, "That means I get the black pencil." Pocket the black pencil and add, ". . . leaving the red pencil for you." Remove the red pencil from under the handkerchief.

If you use a borrowed handkerchief, there is a way to enhance the illusion that the pencil is tearing its way through the handkerchief. When you reach the position of Figure 167 and have curled the left fingers around the handkerchief, pick up a previously formed cone of newspaper with the right hand, Figure 170 and place it over the top of the handkerchief. Cause the pencil apparently to penetrate the handkerchief and the paper as shown in Figure 168. In the spectator's mind, the tearing sound made by the newspaper conjures up the thought that his handkerchief is also being torn.

After the pencil has completed the penetration, allow the torn paper to fall to the table. Crumple up the handkerchief, saying, "No one will notice the tear." Hand it over. The spectator will be surprised to discover that his handkerchief is in one piece.

# VANISHES

Handkerchief vanishes are an important part of handkerchief magic; one of the simplest handkerchief vanishes uses an ordinary newspaper. It is described in this chapter along with another practical method that can be used in many tricks in which it is required to bring about the vanish of a handkerchief in a convincing manner.

## 26. Paper-Bag Vanish

This is an excellent method of vanishing one or more handkerchiefs. It is simple and inexpensive to make, and can be done even when the performer is surrounded by the audience. The following description is based on an article by John Braun.

Needed are brown paper bags, the kind used to bag groceries. The size should be approximately 9½" by 16" and about 6" wide. Obtain several so you can make up duplicate apparatus at one sitting.

Cut out the portion of the bag shown by the dotted lines in Figure 171. Apply paste or glue to the shaded areas of the cut-out panel, Figure 172.

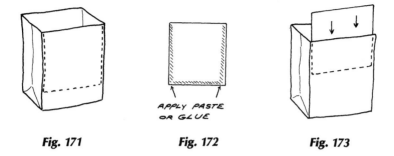

**Fig. 171**          **Fig. 172**          **Fig. 173**

With the glue still wet, slide the panel into an ordinary paper bag, Figure 173. Let the glue dry. The result is that a pocket has been created inside the paper bag, Figure 174.

Fold the bag so it lies flat. Keep it on the table until you are ready to perform the trick. When you are ready to use the paper bag in a trick requiring the vanish of a handkerchief, slide the right thumb into the pocket as you grasp the bag, Figure 175. Snap the bag open, keeping the thumb in place.

**Fig. 174**                    **Fig. 175**

Place a silk into the bag, really placing it into the pocket. Grip the bag again so the right thumb is now outside the pocket, Figure 176. The left hand grasps the front of the bag at the point marked X. Tear open the bag as shown in Figure 177 to show that the handkerchief has vanished. Unknown to the audience, the handkerchief is concealed in the pocket.

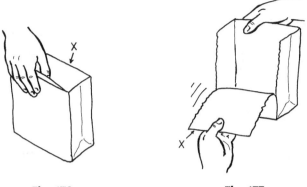

**Fig. 176**                    **Fig. 177**

One simple use for the paper-bag vanisher is to seem to drop a silk into the bag, shake the bag, then remove the silk to show that you have shaken a knot into the silk. All you need do is have a duplicate silk already at the bottom of the bag prior to performance. This silk has a knot in its center.

Display an unknotted silk and place it into the bag, really placing it into the pocket. Slip the thumb outside the pocket and grip the bag as shown in Figure 176. Shake the bag, then have a spectator reach into the bag and remove the silk. It appears as if you caused a knot to appear in the silk simply by shaking the bag. In this trick the prepared bag was used to switch silks rather than to vanish a silk.

Silk handkerchief have less bulk than handkerchiefs made of other materials. This means that they are better concealed in the compartment in the bag.

## 27.   Silk Spectrum

This is an adaptation of a fine trick by Oswald Rae. A colored silk, freely chosen by the audience, is made to vanish and reappear inside a sealed envelope bearing the spectator's initials.

METHOD: Required is a simple cardboard stand used to display three envelopes. Take a piece of 8½″ by 11″ cardboard and fold it in thirds, Figure 178. Then tape the ends together as shown in Figure 179 to make the stand. The stand can be covered with construction paper to add color.

Use 12″ silks for this trick. Seal a red silk in one envelope, a white silk in another and a blue silk in another. Place the sealed envelopes on the stand as shown in Figure 180.

Also required are duplicate red, white and blue silks. These are on display at the beginning of the trick.

The final item of apparatus is the paper-bag vanisher, prepared with the pocket as already explained (No. 26). Inside, at the bottom of the bag, are two empty sealed envelopes.

To perform the trick, have the spectator choose one of the three displayed envelopes. Say he picks the one in the middle. Unknown to him, there is a white silk inside this sealed envelope. Ask the spectator for his initials. Jot them down on the flap of the envelope. Then drop this envelope into the paper bag. Remove the other two envelopes from the stand and drop them into the bag, but make sure they go into the pocket.

Display the three silks. Drop the red silk and blue silk into the bag but place the white silk into the pocket. Shake up the bag, then tear it open. Three envelopes plus the red and blue silks are seen to fall from the bag. The white silk has vanished.

Tear open each of the two empty envelopes to show them empty. Then have the spectator tear open the envelope bearing his initials. The white silk is found inside this envelope.

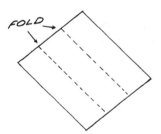

Fig. 178

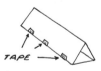

Fig. 179

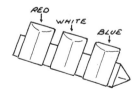

Fig. 180

## 28.    An Impromptu Vanisher

An excellent silk vanisher can be made from a newspaper. It can vanish one 18″ silk or two 12″ silks. The following is the first complete description of the handling to appear in print.

Use a full-size newspaper, not a tabloid. When spread out flat, a full-size sheet will measure about 27½″ by 21¾″. Stack four sheets on top of one another. Fold them in half along the center fold. This will bring you to the position of Figure 181. Fold the paper in half from right to left, Figure 182.

Beginning at the upper-right corner, mark off a distance of 6½″ along the top edge and 9″ along the right side edge. This is shown in Figure 182-A. Using a ruler or the edge of the table, put a crease in the paper as shown by the dotted lines in Figure 182-A. This brings you to the situation of Figure 183.

From this point you will wrap the cone around on itself. To begin, use X-X as a fold line. Fold the portion on the right of X-X over to the left. You are now at the situation of Figure 184. Using Y-Y as a fold line, fold the portion to the right of Y-Y over to the left. This brings you to the position shown in Figure 185.

To complete the formation of the cone, fold the small portion at the bottom of the cone over in the direction of the arrow in Figure 185. The cone should look like Figure 186. Press the cone flat.

Fold the top corners down in the direction of the arrow in Figure 186. Lift up all but two of the corners, Figure 187.

To vanish one or more silks, hold the cone in the left hand. The right side of the body is toward the audience. Open out the mouth of

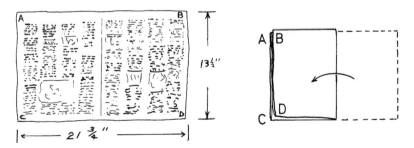

Fig. 181                                      Fig. 182

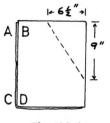

**Fig. 182-A**

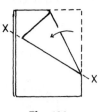

**Fig. 183**

**Fig. 184**

**Fig. 185**

**Fig. 186**

**Fig. 187**

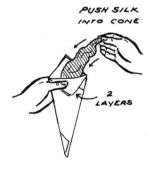

PUSH SILK INTO CONE

2 LAYERS

**Fig. 188**

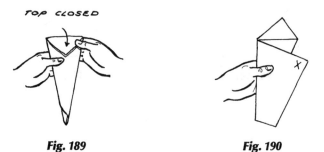

**Fig. 189**                    **Fig. 190**

the cone, then tuck the silk down inside, Figure 188. Close the top of the cone, Figure 189. Tap the cone against the tabletop.

To open the cone, release the right hand's grip on the right side of the cone. This allows the cone to open out as shown in Figure 190.

Reach behind the upper portion and grasp the cone as shown by the dotted lines in Figure 191. The left hand then grasps the right side of the newspaper at the corner marked X and opens the paper to the left, Figure 192.

The right hand releases its grip, allowing the newspaper to open on the right side. The right hand then regrips the right side of the paper at the bottom as shown in Figure 193.

The left thumb then reaches into the center of the paper, Figure 194. The right thumb also reaches into the center, Figure 195. The newspaper is opened out, Figure 196, to show the complete vanish of the silk. When performing the vanish, stand so the right side is toward the audience. Thus, their view of the apparatus is that depicted in Figures 190–196.

Once the handling is learned, this is a baffling vanish of a silk. The silk can be apparently reproduced by following the vanish with "Silk from Silk" (No. 16). A good routine can be devised by poking a silk into the newspaper cone with a pen, then tossing in the pen as an afterthought. Open the newspaper to show the articles have vanished. Then fold the newspaper in half and place it aside. Borrow a handkerchief and seemingly produce the vanished silk and pen by the method described in "A Novel Production" (No. 15).

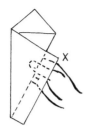

Fig. 191

Fig. 192

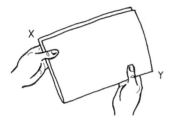

Fig. 193

Fig. 194

Fig. 195

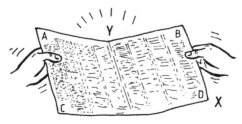

Fig. 196

# SYMPATHETIC SILKS

Early in the present century, Hatton and Plate introduced one of the best new ideas in handkerchief magic. Writing in *Magicians' Tricks and How They Are Done* (1910), they described an effect in which three separate handkerchiefs were rolled into balls and tossed into the air. When the handkerchiefs descended it was seen that they were knotted together. The handkerchiefs were tossed into the air again, and descended separate once more.

Three years later, Edward Victor and G. W. Hunter added the "sympathy" angle, in which one group of handkerchiefs was shown to act in sympathy with another. Two of the best routines exploiting this theme are described in this chapter.

## 29. Think Alike

Three handkerchiefs of different colors are shown and draped onto a bag, Figure 197. The tops of the handkerchiefs are always in view. A duplicate set of handkerchiefs is shown to the audience. A spectator chooses one. He has a free choice. A knot is tied in the end of this handkerchief. The handkerchief of the same color is lifted from the bag, and now it too has a knot tied in it, Figure 198.

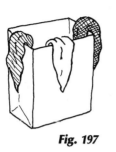

Fig. 197

Fig. 198

The effect can be repeated with each of the remaining handkerchiefs.

METHOD: This fine routine was devised by Edward Bagshawe. Required are three sets of 18″ handkerchiefs and an ordinary paper bag. Assume the handkerchiefs consist of three reds, three whites and three blues.

Place a red handkerchief on the table, Figure 199. Tie a knot near end A, Figure 200. Fold end B down to meet end D along the dotted line shown in Figure 200.

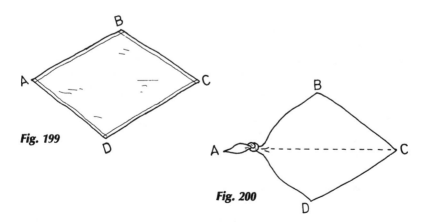

Fig. 199

Fig. 200

The situation is shown in Figure 201. Fold the handkerchief in half along the dotted line shown in Figure 201. The result is shown in Figure 202.

Imagine the handkerchief to be divided into thirds as shown by X–X and Y–Y in Figure 203. Grasp the handkerchief at X–X with both hands and bring X–X over to the position shown in Figure 204.

Finally, fold the handkerchief in half the long way, bringing you to the situation of Figure 205. Place the folded red handkerchief against another red handkerchief, Figure 206. Fold end E down to meet end H, Figure 207. This completes the preparation of one pair of red handkerchiefs.

Repeat this procedure with a pair of white handkerchiefs and a pair of blue handkerchiefs. Place the prepared handkerchiefs on top of one another.

To present the trick, grasp the prepared handkerchiefs at the upper ends. Remove the red handkerchief, Figure 208, and place it in the bag, but keep the upper end in view. Drape this end over the top of the bag. Do the same thing with the white handkerchief, and then the blue handkerchief. The handkerchiefs now appear as shown in Figure 197.

Pick up the third set of handkerchiefs. Let the audience choose one. Say they choose the white handkerchief. Openly tie a knot in it. Then explain that this handkerchief will cause the white handkerchief in the bag to act in sympathy. Grasp the upper end of the white handkerchief in the bag and lift it out of the bag, Figure 198, to show that this handkerchief now has a knot tied in it.

Harold Rice suggested repeating the trick. Have the spectator choose either of the remaining handkerchiefs. Say he chooses blue. Tie a knot in the blue handkerchief. Then lift the duplicate blue handkerchief out of the bag to show that it too now has a knot tied in it. Finally, tie a knot in the remaining handkerchief, in this case the red. Then lift the red handkerchief out of the bag to show that it is now knotted.

The trick works on the premise that each handkerchief consists of an outer shell that conceals an already knotted handkerchief. When each of the prepared handkerchiefs is placed in the bag, the outer shell falls away, so that the knotted handkerchief may be lifted out of the bag. The fold of Figures 199–203 is designed to make the outer handkerchief fall away rapidly.

Depending on the type of handkerchief you use, you may find that

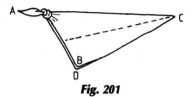

Fig. 201

Fig. 202

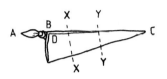

Fig. 203

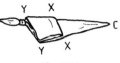

Fig. 204

Fig. 205

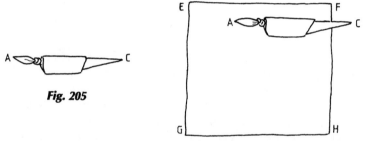

Fig. 206

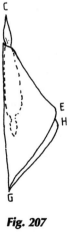

Fig. 207

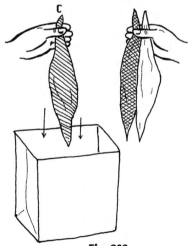

Fig. 208

the outer handkerchief does not always fall away. To protect against this, cut a window in the bottom of the bag, Figure 209. You can then check visually that each of the outer handkerchiefs has fallen to the bottom of the bag. If one has not, then you can use the following maneuver.

**Fig. 209**    WINDOW

Place the left hand at the bottom of the bag in back, as if to steady the bag, while the right hand lifts the proper handkerchief out. In fact, the left hand reaches into the window and grasps the outer handkerchief, thus anchoring it in place. The right hand then lifts the corresponding knotted handkerchief out of the bag.

The effect can be varied in different ways. For example, when preparing the handkerchiefs, tie two knots in the white handkerchief. The knots should be a few inches apart. When you are performing the routine, if the spectator chooses white, tie two knots in the unprepared handkerchief. Then reach into the bag, remove the white handkerchief and show two knots in it.

When presenting the trick, take the red or blue handkerchief first. Tie a single knot in the handkerchief. Then lift the corresponding handkerchief from the bag to show that it too has a knot. Now repeat the effect with the white handkerchief but, as a seeming afterthought, tie an extra knot in the white handkerchief. When the white handkerchief is removed from the paper bag, it has two knots tied in it.

### 30. Sympathetic Silks

Commenting on this routine, Harlan Tarbell wrote, "A beautiful problem with silks. A great favorite of Houdini. In various forms, this problem has graced the acts of a number of professionals."

Six separate handkerchiefs are shown. Three are placed on a chair in full view. The other three are tied together in a chain. The performer remarks that a sympathy exists between the silks. Because the magician tied three of the silks together, the other three silks will tie themselves together. The three separate handkerchiefs are lifted from the chair, but now they are tied together.

The magician unties these three handkerchiefs. Because of the sympathetic bond, the other three handkerchiefs instantly untie themselves!

METHOD: This is the simplest method of performing "Sympathetic Silks." Required are six 18″ cotton or silk handkerchiefs.

This routine uses two handkerchief principles that have many uses. One principle is a false count that allows you to show six apparently separate silks. The other is a false knot known as a Twist Away Knot; the knot appears genuine but will dissolve almost instantly.

Tie three of the handkerchiefs together as shown in Figure 210. Bring the knots in toward the center of the middle handkerchief. Place a single handkerchief to the left of the knotted group of three, and two single handkerchiefs to the right. The six handkerchiefs are placed on a table or chair in the condition shown in Figure 211.

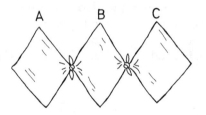

**Fig. 210**

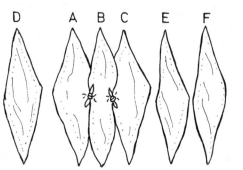

**Fig. 211**

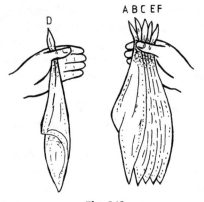

**Fig. 212**

To present the routine, pick up all six handkerchiefs with the right hand. You are going to count the handkerchiefs from hand to hand to show that you seem to have six single handkerchiefs. On the count of one, take handkerchief D into the left hand, Figure 212.

On the count of two, take handkerchief A, but keep the hands together as shown in Figure 213. On the count of three, take handkerchief B, and on the count of four take handkerchief C. Make sure the hands remain fairly close together for the handkerchiefs taken on the count of two, three, four.

On the count of five, take handkerchief E, as in Figure 214, pulling

**Fig. 213**

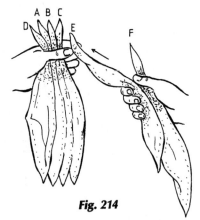

**Fig. 214**

it through the right fingers as it is taken to the left. On the count of six, give handkerchief F a shake to emphasize that it is a single handkerchief, then take it in the left hand. Practice is required to learn the count so it can be done smoothly and without hesitation.

Transfer all six handkerchiefs to the right hand. Then grasp corners A, B, C of the tied-together group and take them in the left hand, Figure 215. Place them in full view on a table or chair as you say, "We'll leave these three handkerchiefs here."

You are going to tie the remaining three handkerchiefs together using the Twist Away Knot. Place one of the single handkerchiefs over the other as shown in Figure 216. In this and subsequent drawings, one handkerchief will be shown shaded to make the knot-tying sequence easier to follow. In actual performance all handkerchiefs are the same color.

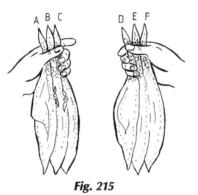

**Fig. 215**

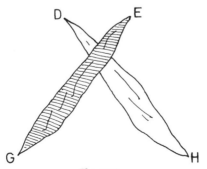

**Fig. 216**

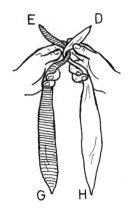

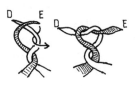

**Fig. 218**

**Fig. 217**

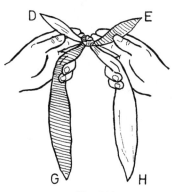

**Fig. 219**

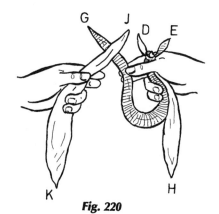

**Fig. 220**

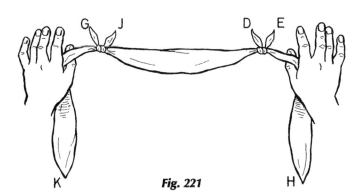

**Fig. 221**

Twist the ends around one another, bringing you to the situation of Figure 217. Bring end E over end D, Figure 218. Then bring end E around behind the other handkerchief and through the loop as shown by the arrows in Figure 218. The result is the knot shown in Figure 219. Pull the ends tight.

Place the knot just formed between the right thumb and first finger. The left hand then aids in bringing the other end of the shaded handkerchief to a position between the right thumb and first finger. The left hand then places the upper end of its remaining single handkerchief against the upper end of the shaded handkerchief. The position is shown in Figure 220. Tie ends G and J together using the Twist Away Knot. Pull the knot tight.

Display the chain of handkerchiefs by letting the end handkerchiefs rest on the thumbs, Figure 221. Point the thumbs toward each other, Figure 222. Then allow the handkerchief on the right to slide off your right thumb onto the left thumb, Figure 223.

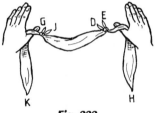

**Fig. 222**

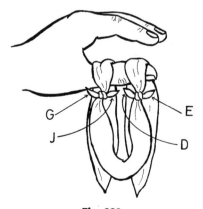

**Fig. 223**

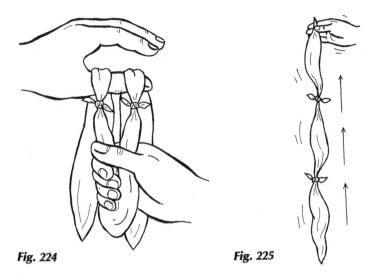

**Fig. 224**　　　　　　　　**Fig. 225**

Grasp the middle handkerchief with the right hand as shown in Figure 224. As you do, say to the audience, "We've knotted these three handkerchiefs together, and we'll leave them over here."

Close the left hand around the two end handkerchiefs. As you place these three handkerchiefs on the table some distance away from the other set of handkerchiefs, pull the end handkerchiefs back with the left hand. The right hand maintains its grip on the middle handkerchief. The result is that the Twist Away Knots will be upset and the handkerchiefs will be free of each other. Because you hold the handkerchiefs as indicated in Figure 224, the two end handkerchiefs hide the middle handkerchief from audience view. The audience is therefore unaware that these handkerchiefs are no longer knotted.

As you place the handkerchiefs down, say, "The handkerchiefs act in sympathy. These three are knotted. In a split second, those three loose handkerchiefs will knot themselves."

Walk over to where the first set of three handkerchiefs were placed. Grasp one end and pull them with a snapping motion. They will be displayed in a chain as shown in Figure 225.

Wait for the effect to register. When the applause subsides, say, "It works in reverse, too." Openly untie the chain of three handkerchiefs. Display them singly and drop them on the table. Then walk over to where the second set was placed. Say, "It has happened already. These three handkerchiefs have untied themselves."

Lift the handkerchiefs one at a time to show that they are now untied.

# THE MOUSE

## 31. The Mouse

This chapter is devoted to a handkerchief fold where one can transform a handkerchief into an animated mouse. Martin Gardner calls the mouse "the greatest of all hank folds." Made from an ordinary cotton handkerchief, the mouse wiggles its tail, hops up the magician's arm and even jumps into a child's lap. The following description, made available by Martin Gardner, is the first complete account to appear in print.

Use an 18" white cotton handkerchief. A table napkin may also be used. Spread the handkerchief out flat on the table, Figure 226. Bring end D up to meet end A, Figure 227. Then fold ends B and C toward the middle, overlapping the ends about 2 to 4" as in Figure 228.

A triangle is formed with the overlapping corners A–D at the top and corners E and F at the base. Roll up the lower part of the handkerchief until it reaches the top corners of the folds E–F, Figure 229. Turn the handkerchief over from top to bottom to arrive at the situation shown in Figure 230.

Fold ends E and F toward the center so they overlap about an inch, Figure 231. Then tuck ends A and D down inside the opening as shown in Figure 232.

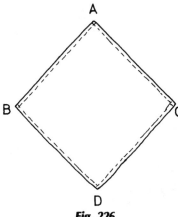

*Fig. 226*

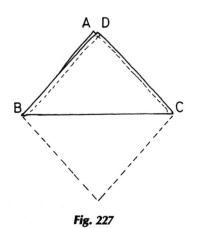

*Fig. 227*

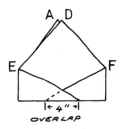

*Fig. 228*

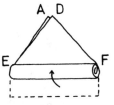

*Fig. 229*

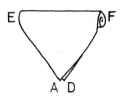

*Fig. 230*

*Fig. 231*

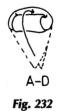

*Fig. 232*

Insert the thumbs into the pocket, Figure 233. Roll the handkerchief over in the direction indicated by the arrows in Figure 234. Continue this rolling maneuver until the ends show, Figure 235. Holding the mouse's body with the right hand, gently pull one end out, Figure 236, then the other. The result is shown in Figure 237.

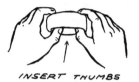

INSERT THUMBS

**Fig. 233**

**Fig. 234**

**Fig. 235**

SLOWLY
PULL ENDS
FREE

**Fig. 236**

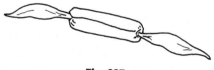

**Fig. 237**

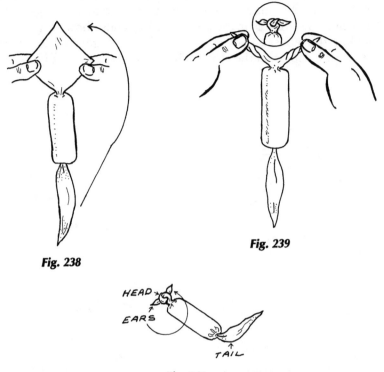

Fig. 238

Fig. 239

Fig. 240

To form the mouse's head and ears, grasp one end between the hands. Flatten it out, Figure 238. Then twirl the body two or three times around this end in the direction shown by the arrow in Figure 238.

The result is shown in Figure 239. Knot the ends together to form the head and ears. The finished product is the mouse, as shown in Figure 240.

To animate the mouse, place it on the left palm as shown in Figure 241. Cup the right hand over the mouse and stroke its back, Figure 242. To make the tail wiggle, jiggle it at its base with the left first or second finger. Another way to make the tail move is to clip it between the left first and second fingers. By moving these fingers, the tail will wave from side to side. Be sure the right hand covers the left fingers as indicated in Figure 242.

To make the mouse jump, snap its body with the curled left fingers. Note that in Figure 241 the four fingers of the left hand, partly curled, are in position to snap the base of the mouse so it will jump up onto your wrist. As soon as it jumps, grab the tail with your right hand, Figure 243, and bring the mouse back to the left palm. Try to time it so the right hand grabs the mouse while the mouse is still in motion. The illusion you want to create is that the mouse is trying to get away.

Make the mouse jump two or three times. Then make it jump completely out of your hand. Properly aimed, the mouse will jump into a child's lap. Take the mouse back, stroke its back as if to quiet it down. Make the mouse jump onto your left arm. Grasp it with the

**Fig. 241**

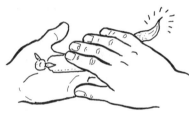

**Fig. 242**

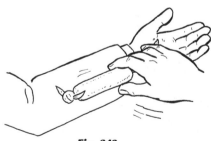

**Fig. 243**

right hand. Pretend that you are trying to drag the mouse back, but use the right hand to bring the mouse to the shoulder, Figure 244. Let the mouse fall back over the left shoulder. Grab it by the tail with the right hand and bring it back into view.

You can make the mouse seem to climb around the neck by acting as though the mouse was trying to get away. Actually, the right hand guides the mouse around the neck. Grasp the mouse with the left hand and bring it back into view.

Magic shops and novelty stores sell a device called a watch winder. It can be concealed in the hand, and produces a noise that imitates the sound of a noisy watch being wound. Stewart Judah suggested using a watch winder in conjunction with the mouse. Hold the mouse in the left hand. Remark that he has to be wound from time to time. Pretend to take an invisible key from the pocket. Actually, when the hand goes into the pocket, it takes the watch winder and conceals it in the palm. Pretend to push the invisible key into to the side of the mouse, then pantomine winding the mouse up. The watch winder, concealed in the hand, makes a realistic and comical winding noise.

You can also use a real key. Place the key between the left fingers. Then pretend to wind the mouse up by twisting the key as shown in Figure 245.

After the mouse goes through more antics, you can make it move slower and slower. Remark that it is winding down. If the mouse does

*Fig. 244*    *Fig. 245*

not perform for a child, explain to the child that the mouse has unwound and needs a rest.

There are several ways to end the demonstration. You can unknot the ears so that the mouse is back to the shape shown in Figure 237. Have two children each make a wish. They each take an end of the mouse and pull. The child whose end unravels first will be the first to get his or her wish.

An ending suggested by the author is this: At the start of the demonstration explain that you have a paper bag containing handkerchiefs. Reach in, remove one handkerchief, look at it and say, "This is the mouse." Make the mouse and animate it as described above. To finish, unknot the ears and drop the mouse back into the bag. Remove handkerchiefs one at a time from the bag. At some point, grasp the mouse and begin lifting it out of the bag with the left hand. The right hand grasps the lower end of the mouse through the bag, Figure 246. As the left hand pulls upward, the mouse, unseen, unfurls.

**Fig. 246**

Place this handkerchief on the table. Then remove the remaining handkerchiefs, one at a time. The audience assumes the mouse is still in the bag. Turn the bag over, or have the spectators peer into the bag to see that the mouse has vanished.

You can have a spectator choose one of the handkerchiefs. Say, "That one is Fatima." Go on from here to produce "Fatima" (No. 54). When another handkerchief is chosen, say, "This is the mouse." By following this procedure you can construct a number of different animated figures.

# SQUARE-KNOT SECRETS

In *The Discoverie of Witchcraft*, author Reginald Scot described one of the earliest-known handkerchief tricks: "Of fast or loose, how to knit a hard knot upon a handkercher, and to undo the same with words."

From 1584, when Scot wrote these words, to the present, false knots have taken their place as being among the fundamental principles of handkerchief magic. The square knot is of particular interest because it is a knot that can be pulled tight by a spectator yet secretly upset or "slipped" in an instant. This chapter details the basic square knot and a number of tricks.

## 32.  The Square Knot

For this discussion we will assume that you use two 18″ handkerchiefs, one red and one white. This is to make the handling clear in the diagrams. In actual performance you would use two handkerchiefs of the same color.

Hold one handkerchief in each hand, the red in the left. Hold each handkerchief about 4″ from the top. Then cross the right handkerchief over the left, Figure 247.

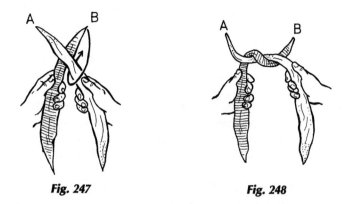

Fig. 247                          Fig. 248

The first knot is tied by threading end B in the direction of the arrow shown in Figure 247. The result is shown in Figure 248.

Cross the left end over the right end, Figure 249. Then form the second knot by bringing end A around end B in the direction shown by the arrow in Figure 249. The result is the square knot of Figure 250. Pull the knot snug. This is done by pulling end B to the left with the left fingers and end A to the right with the right fingers. Do not pull the knot too tight.

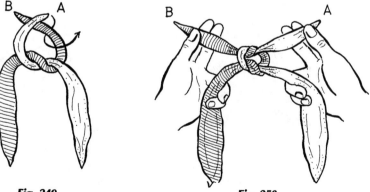

Fig. 249                          Fig. 250

It is easy to remember how to form a square knot. Remember: right over left (Figure 247), then left over right (Figure 249). The square knot has the feature that if you pull the handkerchiefs in opposite directions in an effort to pull them apart, no matter how hard you pull, the knot only tightens. But the square knot can be upset or dissolved if the secret is known. It is done in the following way.

After forming the square knot of Figure 250, pretend to tighten the knot in the manner described here. Firmly grip the knot itself between the left thumb and forefinger. The right hand then takes end A and pulls it outward, Figure 251. Since the left thumb has closed down over the knot, the knot cannot tighten. The audience is unaware of this, so when they see you pull on end A, they think the knot is being drawn tighter. Make it look genuine by grimacing, as though you are using force to tighten the knot.

You now pretend to tighten the other end of the knot and it is here that the secret action takes place. Bring the left hand back so it is behind the knot. The right hand then grips end B and pulls it with steadily increasing pressure, Figure 252. You will find that the knot changes. The right-hand handkerchief is now knotted *around* the end of the left-hand handkerchief, Figure 253.

To release the handkerchiefs from one another, grip the right-hand handkerchief at the knot with the right hand. Then pull the left-hand handkerchief free, Figure 254, by sliding it off the other handkerchief.

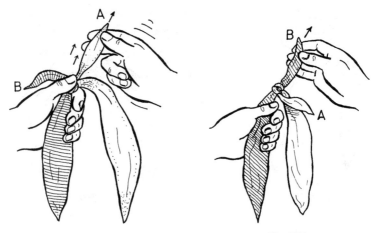

**Fig. 251**                    **Fig. 252**

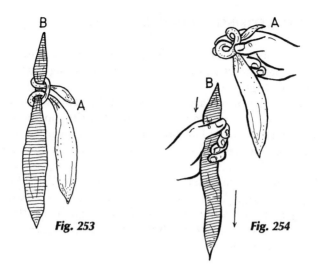

**Fig. 253**          **Fig. 254**

## 33.   Teach In

Two handkerchiefs are knotted together, Figure 255, and are dropped into a paper bag so the ends are in view, Figure 256. Two other handkerchiefs are knotted together. The magician remarks that these handkerchiefs will teach the ones in the bag how to free themselves from one another.

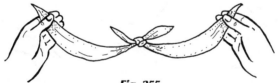

**Fig. 255**

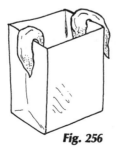

**Fig. 256**

The two handkerchiefs in hand magically unknot. Immediately the other handkerchiefs are removed from the bag. Now they too are unknotted, Figure 257.

METHOD: Required are four 18″ handkerchiefs and a paper bag. The bag should measure about 6″ by 9″ at the top and about 16″ in depth. Knot two of the handkerchiefs together using the square-knot handling of Figures 247–250. Upset the square knot by the handling of Figures 251 and 252.

Place the handkerchiefs into the bag, Figure 258. The right hand steadies the bag. As the handkerchiefs are lowered into the bag, pretend to have trouble getting them to go in neatly. Grasp the handkerchiefs at the knot with the right hand, Figure 259, and lower the right hand into the bag.

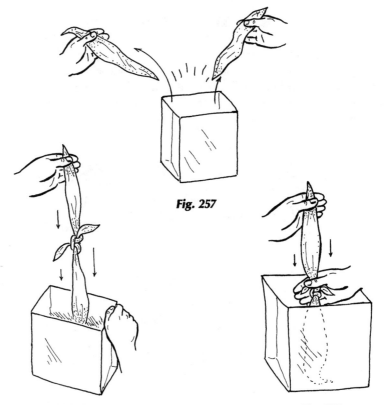

Fig. 257

Fig. 258

Fig. 259

**Fig. 260**

When the right hand has been lowered about 10" into the bag, keep it motionless and bring the left hand upward with the handkerchief it holds. The result is that the left-hand handkerchief slides free of the other handkerchief.

The left hand drapes its handkerchief over the left top edge of the bag. Bring the right hand out of the bag. Then, as if it were an afterthought, reach into the bag with the right hand and bring an end of the other handkerchief out. Drape it over the top edge of the bag on the right side. The situation is as shown in Figure 256. The audience assumes the handkerchiefs are firmly knotted together.

Pick up the other two handkerchiefs and knot them together using the Twist Away Knot described in "Sympathetic Silks" (No. 30). Place the knotted handkerchiefs over your shoulders. Pull them apart with a gentle motion, Figure 260. Then explain that the handkerchiefs inside the bag learn how to free themselves by watching. Take a handkerchief in each hand and gently remove them from the bag, Figure 257.

## 34.  Dissolvo

Two handkerchiefs are knotted together and placed into a glass. The magician snaps his fingers. Slowly the handkerchiefs are removed. The knots have dissolved.

This routine is based on a flawless handling devised by Slydini.

METHOD: For maximum visibility use two brightly colored 27" handkerchiefs and a stemmed glass large enough to hold the handkerchiefs.

Tie the handkerchiefs together using the square knot. Upset the knot with the handling of Figures 251 and 252. Drape the handkerchiefs over the palm of the right hand, Figure 261. Bring the palm-up left hand to a position just under the right hand, between the right hand and the lower handkerchief. The left hand moves up to the position shown in Figure 262. The left hand spreads the upper handkerchief as it reaches the position shown in Figure 262.

The right thumb is placed directly on top of the knot. The left thumb is placed on the upper handkerchief at a point just above the knot, Figure 263.

As the audience sees the following handling, it seems that you use the left-hand handkerchief to cover the knot. What actually happens is this: While the right hand remains motionless, the left hand brings its handkerchief upward. As shown in Figure 264, the left-hand handkerchief slides free of the other handkerchief; it is pulled from the stationary handkerchief while moving upward. Because the upper handkerchief has been spread, the cloth hides or screens the action from audience view.

As soon as the upper handkerchief is free, drape it over the other handkerchief, Figure 265.

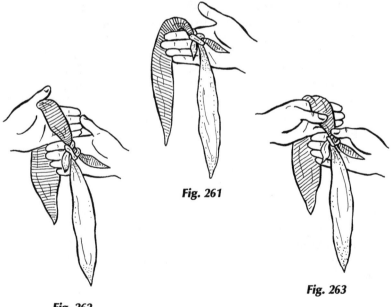

**Fig. 261**

**Fig. 262**

**Fig. 263**

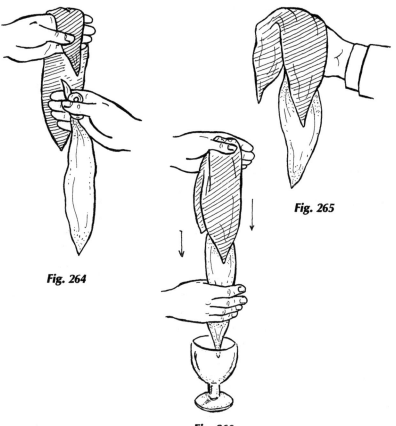

Fig. 265

Fig. 264

Fig. 266

Grasp both handkerchiefs at the top with the left hand. Using the right hand to guide the handkerchiefs, tuck them into a glass, Figure 266.

Snap the fingers. Slowly pull the handkerchiefs out of the glass, one at a time, to show that the knot has dissolved.

The trick can be done with a single handkerchief. Use a 27″ handkerchief for maximum visibility. Tie diagonally opposite corners together with a square knot. As you do, patter to the effect that the handkerchief is one that belonged to the assistant of a great escape artist and that it remembers how to free itself from bonds. Upset the knot. Then slip the ends free of one another as you bring the center of the handkerchief up to cover the knot.

To finish, grasp adjacent corners of the handkerchief and shake it out to show that the knot has mysteriously dissolved.

### 35.   Switch Over

The magician shows a red handkerchief knotted to a white hand-kerchief. In his other hand he holds another white handkerchief, Figure 267. The red handkerchief is pulled free and placed aside. But now the two white handkerchiefs are seen to be knotted together, Figure 268.

In the literature of square-knot tricks, this routine is one of the most offbeat. It was invented by Sid Miller and Sol Hirsh.

METHOD: One red handkerchief and two white handkerchiefs are used. Silk works better than cotton, but you may find that the trick works well with a red silk handkerchief and two white cotton handkerchiefs.

To tie the knot, place one end of a white handkerchief over an end of the red handkerchief, Figure 269. Bring end B around in the direction of the arrow in Figure 269. The result is shown in Figure 270.

Now cross end A over end B, Figure 271. To complete the square knot, bring end A around end B in the direction indicated by the arrow in Figure 271. Pull the ends snug. The result is the square knot of Figure 272.

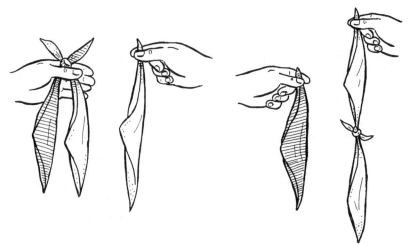

Fig. 267                                    Fig. 268

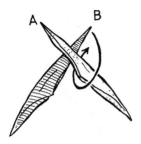

Fig. 269

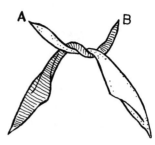

Fig. 270

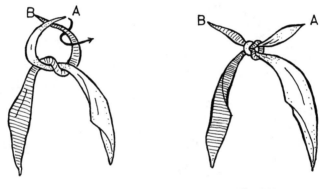

Fig. 271                    Fig. 272

To complete the preparation for this effect, the square knot is upset by pulling the end of the red handkerchief upward and the body of the red handkerchief downward, Figure 273. The situation at this point is that the white handkerchief is knotted around the red handkerchief, Figure 274. The knotting of the two handkerchiefs can be done in front of the audience. Take care to keep the condition of the upset knot from audience view.

To present the routine, hold the knotted handkerchiefs in the left hand, the other white handkerchief in the right, Figure 275. Twist the upper end of the white handkerchief, Figure 276. Place it against the upper end of the red handkerchief, Figure 277.

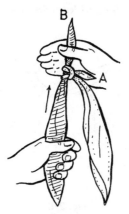

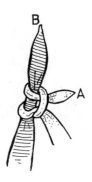

**Fig. 273**

**Fig. 274**

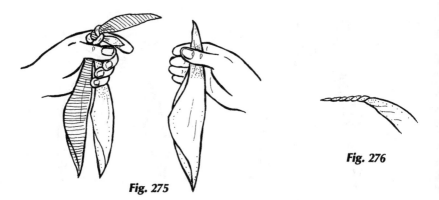

**Fig. 275**

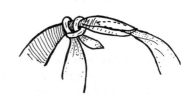

**Fig. 276**

**Fig. 277**

**Fig. 278**

**Fig. 279**

**Fig. 280**

**Fig. 281**

Twist the end of the red handkerchief around the end of the white handkerchief so that the white end is completely enclosed inside the red end, Figure 278. An alternate way of accomplishing this is to twist the ends around one another, Figure 279. Try both ways to see which works better for you.

Hold the handkerchiefs as shown in Figure 280. The right hand holds the portion where the end of the red handkerchief has been wrapped around the white handkerchief. Grasp the knot with the right thumb and first finger, Figure 281.

Pull the red handkerchief downward in the direction shown by the arrow in Figure 281, until it is free of the white handkerchief. As the end of the red handkerchief is pulled through the knot, it will draw the end of the right-hand handkerchief into the knot. The result is that the two white handkerchiefs will be knotted together as shown in Figure 268.

To ensure that the right-hand handkerchief will be pulled into the knot, see to it that the square knot is snug but not too tight. When pulling the red handkerchief downward as shown in Figure 281, do it in a smooth, continuous motion. The trick works better with silk because silk has less bulk than cotton, and a silk handkerchief will slide through the knot more easily than cotton.

When presenting the trick, you can patter to the effect that there were once two lovers, represented by the two white handkerchiefs. One of them strayed momentarily and thought about tying the knot with a redhead. Here you display the red and white handkerchiefs knotted together. But the story had a happy ending. Perform the transfer, ending with the two white handkerchiefs knotted together.

## 36.  Releaso

Jacob Daley devised this beautiful platform trick. The magician knots three silk handkerchiefs together to form a chain. The knotted ends are pushed down into two glasses, Figure 282.

The magician slowly pulls one of the end handkerchiefs upward. It lifts away smoothly, now completely free of the handkerchief it was knotted to a moment before. The end of the handkerchief is not curled or bent. The effect is repeated with the other handkerchief. It too slides free.

**Fig. 282**

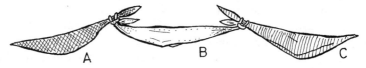

**Fig. 283**

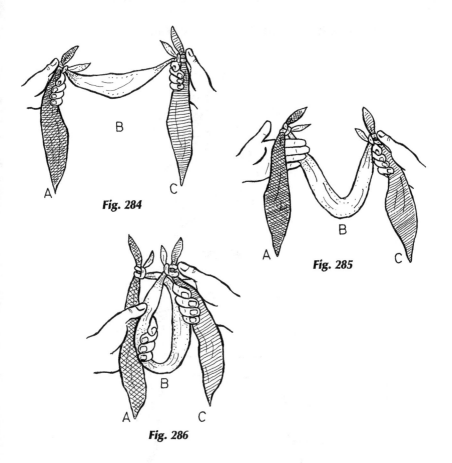

**Fig. 284**

**Fig. 285**

**Fig. 286**

METHOD: Required are three silk handkerchiefs 18″ or larger, and two drinking glasses. The glasses are stacked, mouth up, on the table. In practice the silks should be the same color. In the following illustrations they will be shown in different colors to make the handling clear.

Stand to the left of the table. Tie silks A and B together using a square knot. Secretly upset the knot as you pretend to make the knot tighter. Upset the knot so that the corner of silk A is straight. Then tie silk B to silk C with a square knot. Upset the knot so the corner of C is straight. The situation is shown in Figure 283. The straight ends of the knots belong to the outside silks.

Display the knotted silks as shown in Figure 284. The fingers curl around the outside silks. Bring the hands together, Figure 285, so that the center silk is behind the left hand. Grasp the center silk with the left hand as shown in Figure 286.

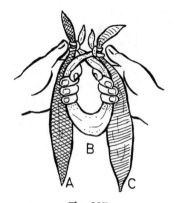

*Fig. 287*

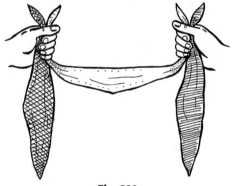

*Fig. 288*

*Fig. 289*

**Fig. 290**

The right hand now releases its grip on the silks. The right hand places the glasses about 12″ apart on the table. Then the right hand grips silks B and C as shown in Figure 287. As you turn to the right to place the silks into the glasses, draw the hands apart, Figure 288.

Both knots will automatically dissolve. The hands hold the ends as shown in Figure 288, so it appears as if the silks are still knotted. The apparently knotted corners are stuffed into the two glasses, Figure 282. Snap the fingers, then slowly draw each of the end silks out to show that the knots have mysteriously dissolved.

The reason the trick works is as follows. Refer to Figure 289. When the knots are tied originally, end X of the center silk is on the left, end Y on the right. When the silks are brought together in Figure 286, the center silk is coiled. This is shown in Figure 289, in which the hands have been removed for clarity. When the silks are drawn apart, end X of the center silk will be on the right, end Y on the left. Thus the ends are exchanged, and it is in this process that the knots are secretly dissolved.

When each square knot is upset, make sure that no more than 1″ of each straight silk protrudes, as indicated in Figure 290. The knots will then dissolve in a quick, indetectable manner.

The trick can be presented as one in which the magician (represented by the center silk) is handcuffed by two unsavory types (as depicted by the end silks). Being a magician, he has no trouble escaping from their clutches.

Another approach is to present the trick as a demonstration of a chain reaction. Tie the silks together to form a chain. Secretly upset the knots. Then tuck the silks into the two glasses. Snap the fingers over the glasses. Then toss the loose silks one at a time into the air.

# PSYCHIC SILKS

In centuries past, magic was linked to the supernatural; one or more psychic tricks were regularly featured in performances of magic for the public. Harlan Tarbell wrote, "Mental mysteries have always been popular in magic because they seem to lift magical effects out of the ordinary and into the realm of the mind." This chapter describes a number of mental and psychic tricks using handkerchiefs.

## 37. Instanto

Houdini's escape tricks were so spectacular, it was speculated he used supernatural powers to dematerialize, and was thus able to free himself from the sturdiest bonds.

This trick has something of the aura of a Houdini escape. The magician's wrists are secured by knotting a handkerchief around them, Figure 293. A spectator standing alongside the magician can verify that the knot is genuine. The magician turns around in a complete circle. When he faces front again, the magician's hands are free, Figure 296.

The magician turns full circle again. When he faces front, his

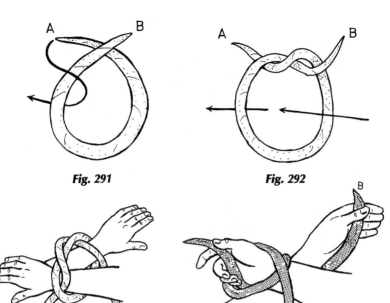

Fig. 291

Fig. 292

Fig. 293

Fig. 294

hands are seen to be genuinely bound by the handkerchief, Figure 293.

METHOD: Invite a spectator up to act as a witness that all is honest and aboveboard. Use a 27" handkerchief. Twirl it ropewise as described in "Threading the Needle" (No. 1). Stand facing the audience so the assisting spectator is alongside you.

Hold an end of the handkerchief in each hand. Cross end B over end A as shown in Figure 291. Bring end A through the loop in the direction of the arrow in Figure 291. This forms the knot shown in Figure 292.

Slide the right hand through the loop in the direction shown by the arrows in Figure 292. Slide the left hand through the loop in back of the right hand. The position of the hands is as shown in Figure 293. Strand B of the handkerchief lies *between* the arms.

Have the spectator tighten the knot a bit. The knot should be snug but not too tight. You need enough room to slide the hands out of the loop. Slowly turn yourself around. When your back is toward the audience, grasp the ends of the handkerchief as shown in Figure 294.

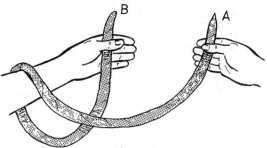

Fig. 295

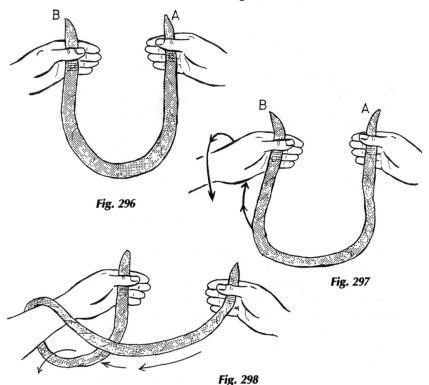

Fig. 296

Fig. 297

Fig. 298

Slide the right hand to the right so it is out of the loop, Figure 295. Then flip the leftmost loop off the left arm. This brings you to the position shown in Figure 296. At this point you should be facing front again. The hands have mysteriously freed themselves from the knot.

To form the knot again, turn slowly around. When your back is toward the audience, flip the center of the rope up onto the left wrist in the direction shown by the arrows in Figure 297.

The rope is now in the position shown in Figure 298. Complete the formation of the knot by sliding the right hand through the loop in the direction of the arrows in Figure 298. Release the ends of the handkerchief. This brings you back to Figure 293. You should time it so you reach this position just as you turn full circle and face front again.

Once you are familiar with the way the handkerchief is knotted over the wrists, you can direct the spectator to do the tying. When learning the trick, make the turn in one smooth, continuous motion. You can increase the speed as you master the handling.

## 38. Matchmaker

In this mental effect the magician and a spectator each get a red, white and blue handkerchief. The magician is blindfolded. He and the spectator stand back to back. The spectator chooses a handkerchief. The blindfolded magician hesitates, then chooses a handkerchief of the same color.

The effect is repeated with the remaining two handkerchiefs. The spectator chooses a handkerchief; the magician unerringly picks a handkerchief of matching color.

METHOD: Since this challenging effect was introduced some years ago, many different methods have been proposed. The one described here uses a confederate. The confederate sits in the front row where the magician can see him.

A set of red, white and blue handkerchiefs is placed over each chair. The magician is blindfolded with an ordinary handkerchief or scarf. Then the magician and the spectator stand back to back as shown in Figure 299.

**Fig. 299**

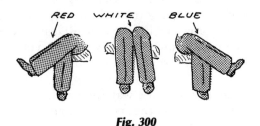

**Fig. 300**

The spectator chooses any handkerchief and holds it over his head with his right hand. As soon as the confederate sees which handkerchief is chosen, he secretly indicates the chosen color to the magician. He does this by the code shown in Figure 300: If red is chosen, the confederate crosses his left leg over his right; if white is chosen, he does not cross his legs; if blue is chosen he crosses his right leg over his left.

**Fig. 301**

The audience is to the magician's right. After the spectator has chosen a handkerchief, the magician turns his head toward the audience. Although he is wearing a blindfold, it is easy for him to peer downward as shown by the arrow in Figure 301. When the magician turns to the audience, he glimpses the position of the confederate's feet and therefore knows the color chosen by the spectator. The magician then holds up the handkerchief of the matching color.

The chosen handkerchiefs are placed aside. Of the two handkerchiefs remaining, the spectator chooses one. The color is tipped off in the same way by the confederate. The magician then picks the handkerchief of the matching color.

As a signal for applause, when the position of Figure 299 is reached the second time, hold up the matching handkerchief in the right hand, face the audience, remove the blindfold with the left hand, and then raise the left hand in the air. With both hands raised you have created a natural signal for applause.

### 39. Match Mates

If you wish to perform "Matchmaker" under impromptu circumstances, the following method devised by the author requires no preparation. The articles may be borrowed. The magician is blindfolded. There is no confederate.

In this trick, each of two spectators gets a red, white and blue handkerchief. The handkerchiefs are randomly mixed, yet the blindfolded magician succeeds in making the colors match.

METHOD: Needed are two red, two white and two blue handkerchiefs. Colored napkins or scarves may also be used. Arrange them in two rows on a table as shown in Figure 302. Each row contains a red, white and blue handkerchief in that order from left to right.

Invite two spectators to assist you. Have one of them blindfold you. Ask spectator 1 to take a place on one side of the table and spectator 2 to stand on the opposite side of the table. The spectators face each other. Turn your back to the table. You are facing the audience. The situation is shown in Figure 303.

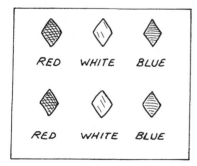

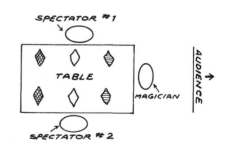

**Fig. 302**                    **Fig. 303**

Ask spectator 2 to exchange any two of his handkerchiefs. Once this has been done it is obvious to the audience that you cannot know the position of any handkerchief in his row.

Have spectator 1 exchange the handkerchief on his right with the middle handkerchief in spectator 2's row. Then have spectator 2 exchange the handkerchief on his right with the middle handkerchief in spectator 1's row. Finally, have spectator 1 pick up his leftmost handkerchief. Have spectator 2 pick up his leftmost handkerchief. These handkerchiefs are exchanged and placed in the vacant positions in the rows. The mixing is now complete.

Ask spectator 1 to pick up the red handkerchief in his row and place it in your left hand. After this is done, hesitate for a moment as if concentrating, then ask spectator 2 to pick up the middle handkerchief in his row and place it in your right hand. Keep both handkerchiefs behind your back so the audience cannot see exactly which colors you have been given.

Ask spectator 1 to pick up the white handkerchief in his row and hold it in his right hand. Pretend to concentrate. Then have spectator 2 pick up the rightmost handkerchief in his row and give it to spectator 1 to hold in his left hand.

Each spectator has one handkerchief remaining. Have spectator 2 take one of these handkerchiefs in each hand.

Remark that, if your powers of psychic deduction are working, you should have correctly paired the colors. Have spectator 1 raise both his hands over his head so the audience can see which handkerchiefs he holds. Say, "Do they match?" He will answer yes.

Have spectator 2 raise both his hands over his head so the audience can see his handkerchiefs. Say, "And if I'm correct again, both of those colors should match, right?" These colors also match.

Then say, "That means I should be holding two red handkerchiefs." Raise both your hands over your head. Bow to the applause.

As an example of how the exchanges might be made, start with the handkerchiefs in the position of Figure 302. Spectator 2 might elect to exchange his blue and white handkerchiefs. After the exchange, the layout will be as shown in Figure 304.

When spectator 1 exchanges the handkerchief on his right with the middle handkerchief in spectator 2's row, the layout will be as shown in Figure 305. After spectator 2 exchanges the handkerchief on *his* right with the middle handkerchief in spectator 1's row, the layout will be as shown in Figure 306.

Finally, after spectator 1's leftmost handkerchief is exchanged with

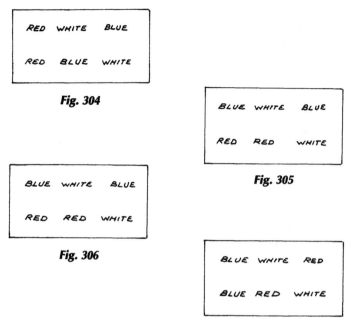

Fig. 304

Fig. 305

Fig. 306

Fig. 307

spectator 2's leftmost handkerchief, the layout will be as shown in Figure 307. Although the process appears random, after all the exchanges have been made, the handkerchiefs in front of spectator 2 will always be in blue-red-white order. This is the key to the working.

## 40. Triple Prophecy

The magician shows that he has a red, a white and a blue handkerchief in a hat, cardboard box or paper bag. He explains that the handkerchiefs are tied together in a particular order.

The spectator is given a matching set of three handkerchiefs. He ties them together in any order, Figure 308. The magician removes the other set of handkerchiefs from the box, Figure 309. They are in exactly the same order!

There are no gimmicks or extra handkerchiefs. The spectator has a free choice of how he arranges his three handkerchiefs.

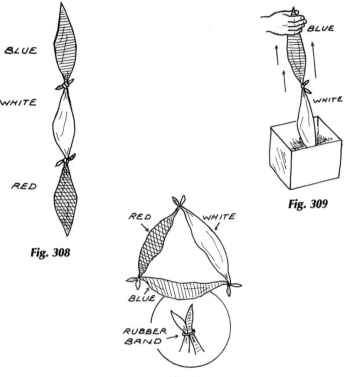

**Fig. 308**

**Fig. 309**

**Fig. 310**

METHOD: Just the two sets of handkerchiefs are used. To prepare the trick, arrange one set of red, white and blue handkerchiefs in a loop by fastening the ends together with small rubber hands, Figure 310. Place this set in the hat, box or bag.

When presenting the trick, tip the hat, box or bag so the audience gets a glimpse of the three handkerchiefs inside. Remark that the handkerchiefs are tied together in a particular order. Say that you will use mental radio waves to try to influence the spectator to choose the same order.

Hand the spectator the other set of three handkerchiefs. Have him tie them together in any order. Say he ties them in blue-white-red order from top to bottom.

Reach into the hat with both hands. Separate the blue handkerchief from the red one by pulling them apart. Then grasp the blue handkerchief and pull the chain of three handkerchiefs from the box as shown in Figure 309. These three handkerchiefs match the spectator's. To say it another way, you have apparently caused the spectator to pick the one right way to arrange his three handkerchiefs. The container can be shown empty after the handkerchiefs are removed.

Remember that, to get the silks in the box to match the order chosen by the spectator, you must note the colors of the end silks in the spectators chain of silks (Figure 308). Separate the two silks of the same colors in your set. Then remove the chain of three silks from the box.

## 41.  No Strings

Some psychics can cause inanimate objects to act in strange ways. In this experiment, the magician makes a drinking glass act as though it were lighter than air; the glass magically remains suspended when a knife is thrust down into it. A view of the handkerchief-covered glass in a state of suspension is shown in Figure 311. All apparatus may be left with the audience at the finish.

METHOD: This trick is based on a clever idea of Ken Allen's. A lightweight transparent plastic glass is recommended. A plastic drinking mug may also be used. Snap two rubber bands around the glass as indicated in Figure 312. The rubber bands should be no more than ¼" apart. Cover the glass with an 18" handkerchief. Silk works better than cotton because it has less bulk. The knife should be the type shown in Figure 313, with a blade that is flat at the handle end.

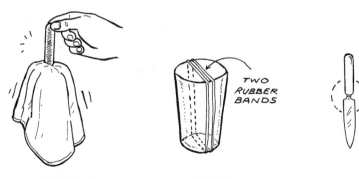

Fig. 311                    Fig. 312                    Fig. 313

**Fig. 314**          **Fig. 315**

When the above preparation has been completed, you are ready to present the routine. Pick up the handkerchief-covered glass with the right hand. The left hand then goes under the handkerchief and grasps the glass at the bottom.

The right hand is now free to pick up the knife from the table. Poke the knife blade down into the glass so the blade slides between the rubber bands. An exposed view, with the handkerchief removed, is shown in Figure 314.

Gently poke the knife down between the rubber bands, pushing the handkerchief in the process, until the blade is below the top of the glass. Then turn the knife 90°. The result is shown in the exposed view of Figure 315; if the left hand is taken away, the glass will be apparently suspended in air. Actually the trick works because the top of the knife blade engages the rubber bands. Display the apparatus as shown in Figure 311. Patter to the effect that the knife is used to hypnotize the glass into thinking it is lighter than air.

To finish, grasp the bottom of the glass with the left hand. Disengage the knife by twisting it so it is parallel to the rubber bands. Place the knife aside. The left third and fourth fingers push the rubber bands off the bottom of the glass as in "A Glass of Helium" (No. 3). The handkerchief is removed and the rubber bands are allowed to fall to the floor. All apparatus may be left with the audience.

You can perform a two-trick routine by preparing a glass as described above. Perform "A Glass of Helium," then follow with "No Strings."

## 42.  Glorpy

John Mulholland wrote, "All those who have seen ghosts are eager to talk about them. Sometimes ghosts have made their presence known without themselves being seen." It is well known that a ghost will slip under a sheet and cavort about by the light of the moon. Displaying an 18″ white handkerchief, the magician remarks that this is the outfit belonging to a baby ghost named Glorpy. The handkerchief is placed flat on the table. A spoon is slipped under the handkerchief. Instantly the spoon begins to stir about and rise off the table as if animated by a ghost. At the finish, the spoon and handkerchief may be left with the audience.

METHOD: You do the trick while seated at a table. There should be a tablecloth on the table. Resting on the knee is a fork, Figure 316. It can be kept in the sock until you are ready to perform. Reach down as if to tie the shoe; in that movement lift the fork out of the sock and put it on the leg with the handle pointing toward the knee.

Borrow two spoons. As this is done, fold the handkerchief or napkin in half. The right hand places the handkerchief on the leg. The fork is secretly taken under the handkerchief, kept in place by the right thumb, Figure 317.

The left hand grasps the other end of the folded handkerchief, Figure 318. The handkerchief is placed on the table as shown in

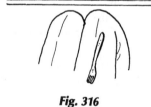

**Fig. 316**

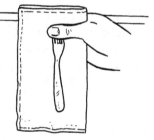

**Fig. 317**

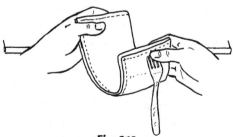

**Fig. 318**

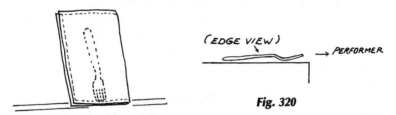

**Fig. 320**

**Fig. 319**

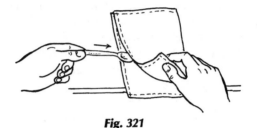

**Fig. 321**

Figure 319. As you place the handkerchief on the table, make sure the left hand keeps its end in contact with the tabletop. This prevents people sitting at the table from catching a glimpse of the fork. In Figure 319 the tines of the fork are near the performer's edge of the table. An edge view is given in Figure 320.

Pick up one of the spoons. Turn it over as if studying it. Place it back on the table. Pick up the other spoon, look it over, appear to be satisfied, then raise one layer of cloth with the right hand and put the spoon between the layers of the handkerchief, Figure 321. The spoon rests near the top of the handle of the fork as shown by the dotted lines in Figure 322.

Stretch out the hands, palm down. The hands move to a position over the handkerchief. The right thumb contacts the tines of the fork, Figure 322. The left hand crosses partway over the right hand so that the left palm conceals the right thumb from audience view, Figure 323, the left fingertips lightly touching the spoon.

By pressing down with the right thumb on the fork, the spoon will appear to levitate. It is a spooky sight. The left fingertips keep the spoon in a horizontal position. A very slight movement of the right thumb against the fork produces a seesaw effect; the handle of the fork rises, causing the handkerchief and the spoon to rise.

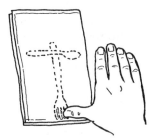

Fig. 322

Fig. 323

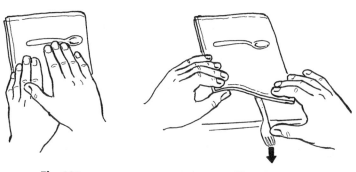

Fig. 324                    Fig. 325

Immediately, release the right thumb's pressure on the fork. The spoon sinks to the table. Change hands, Figure 324. Let the heel of the left thumb rest on the tines of the fork. Use the right fingertips to steady the spoon. Again make the spoon levitate and then slowly sink back.

Remark that the force is sometimes strong enough to levitate two spoons. Place the second spoon on top of the handkerchief so that this spoon is nested in the first spoon. The heel of the left hand contacts the tines of the fork. The right hand is above the left hand with the right fingertips contacting the visible spoon. By pressing down gently on the tines of the fork, both spoons will rise.

Cause the spoons to sink back to the tabletop. Attempt the levitation again, but this time do not make contact with the fork. Pretend to have to make an adjustment. Lift the handkerchief with both hands. With the handkerchief as cover, let the right thumb contact the fork and slide it off the table into the lap, Figure 325.

Remove the visible spoon. The first spoon is still between the layers of cloth. Bring both hands over the handkerchief as shown in Figure 323. This time, allow the right fingertips to touch the bowl of the concealed spoon. There will be a seesaw effect, causing the handle of the spoon to rise upward. Allow it to swing up just a bit, then remark that the ghost needs a rest.

Bring the spoon into view. Leave the apparatus on the table so that curious spectators can look for gimmicks.

At the point shown in Figure 319, do not press the handkerchief out flat on the table. A slightly rumpled condition of the handkerchief will disguise the presence of the fork.

### 43.  Spooky Spoon

A set of silverware from a haunted house is placed on the table, Figure 326. It is covered with a napkin or handkerchief. Immediately a spoon rises up in the air, Figure 327. It cavorts about, then sinks back to the table.

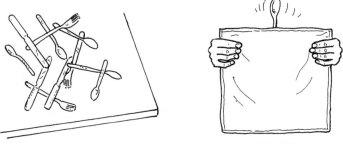

**Fig. 326**                    **Fig. 327**

METHOD: Inexpensive antique-looking spoons, forks and knives can be obtained in rummage shops. Such flatware is not necessary, but adds atmosphere. Seven or eight pieces of flatware are placed in a paper bag. The only secret preparation consists of engaging the handle of a spoon into the tines of a fork as shown in Figure 328. Place this apparatus in the bag, along with an opaque 18″ handkerchief or table napkin.

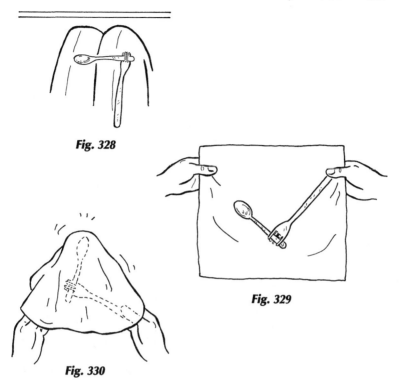

Fig. 328

Fig. 329

Fig. 330

The routine is best done as an after-dinner trick. Place the bag in the lap. Clear a space on the table. Then remove spoons, forks and knives from the bag and place them in a scattered, overlapping arrangement on the table, as in Figure 326. As you do this, at some point, remove the prepared spoon and fork, and place them on the lap, Figure 328 (the view is from above). Then remove the rest of the flatware from the bag and place it on the table. Remove the handkerchief. Hold it stretched between the hands. Keep the hands in the lap as this is done. Secretly grasp the handle of the fork with the right hand. Bring the handkerchief into view as shown in Figure 329.

The flatware on the table is covered with the handkerchief. Make sure the prepared fork and spoon do not contact the other flatware. The right hand pivots at the wrist. This will cause the spoon to pivot to an upright position to a point under the handkerchief, Figure 330. It appears as though one item of cutlery has mysteriously risen off the table.

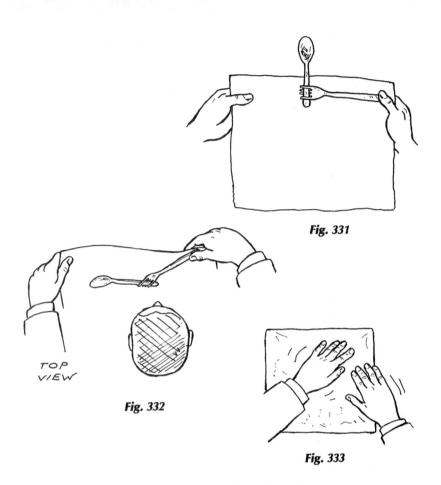

**Fig. 331**

TOP
VIEW

**Fig. 332**

**Fig. 333**

Pretend that the spoon is threatening to rise all the way to the ceiling. Do this by causing the spoon to rise as you act alarmed. To add to the illusion, rise out of the chair as if you are being pulled upward by the spoon. Then pantomime struggling to bring the spoon back.

Return the apparatus to the position shown in Figure 329. Then pivot the fork upward so the spoon rises to a position above the handkerchief, Figure 331. You can bring the spoon back toward the body by bending the right hand at the wrist as in the top view shown in Figure 332.

Allow the spoon to float down behind the handkerchief, Figure 329. Then lower the apparatus to the table so it joins the other flatware. With both hands above the handkerchief, press down on the handkerchief, Figure 333. Remark that you have to do this to keep all of the flatware from rising. In the process, separate the spoon from the fork. Now all may be left for examination.

# TWENTIETH-CENTURY SILKS

British magician Ellis Stanyon once described a trick where one handkerchief vanished and was found between two others previously tied together. Since its appearance in *Conjuring for Amateurs* (1897), this fine trick has come to be known as "Twentieth-Century Silks."

One of the best methods using ordinary handkerchiefs was devised by Lyle Laughlin. In this chapter, a simplified version of the "Twentieth-Century" effect will be described, then a routine that shows how the principle can be used in a different setting, then the classic "Twentieth-Century Silks" using the Laughlin approach.

## 44. Come Back Silk

A handkerchief is given to a spectator to hold. Another handkerchief is placed in a paper cone and vanished. The vanished handkerchief is found to be tied to the end of the handkerchief held by the spectator.

METHOD: Three identical handkerchiefs are used. They can be cotton or silk. It is suggested that white cotton handkerchiefs be used for close-up purposes and brightly colored silk handkerchiefs be used for stage or platform performance.

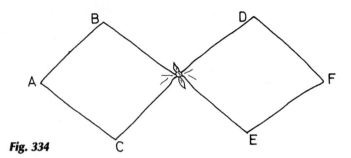

**Fig. 334**

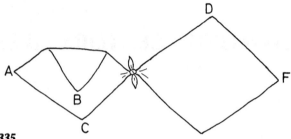

**Fig. 335**

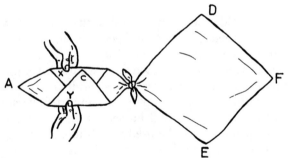

**Fig. 336**

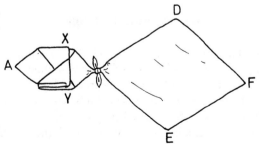

**Fig. 337**

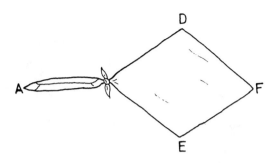

**Fig. 338**

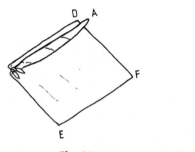

**Fig. 339**

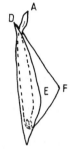

**Fig. 340**

Spread two of the handkerchiefs out on the table. Tie them together as shown in Figure 334. Bring the upper third of the left handkerchief down, Figure 335. Then bring the lower third up as shown in Figure 336. Grasp the left handkerchief at X with the left hand, thumb on top, fingers below. Grasp the handkerchief at Y in a similar way with the right hand. Bring this portion of the handkerchief over to the right. The result is shown in Figure 337.

Roll the left handkerchief in an upward direction, bringing you to the point shown in Figure 338. Because of the rolling of the left handkerchief, the juncture where the handkerchiefs are tied may be twisted. If this happens, smooth out any twists or wrinkles before proceeding.

Bring the rolled handkerchief over onto the other handkerchief, Figure 339. Fold the right handkerchief over onto itself, Figure 340. The rolled handkerchief is now concealed, with only corner A protruding.

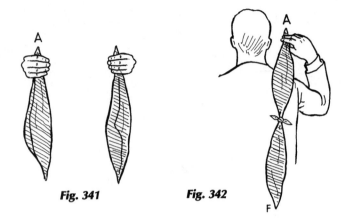

Fig. 341          Fig. 342

To perform the trick, hold the prepared handkerchief in the right hand with corner A protruding above the hand. Hold an unprepared handkerchief in the left hand. The situation is shown in Figure 341.

Ask a spectator to assist. Have him face the audience. Step in back of him and have him grasp corner A of the right-hand handkerchief. Unknown to the spectator and to the audience, as soon as you release your grip on the prepared handkerchief, it will open up as shown in Figure 342. The spectator's body screens this situation from audience view.

Display the other handkerchief. Tuck it into a newspaper cone made up as described in "An Impromptu Vanisher" (No. 28). Tap the newspaper cone against the spectator's shoulder. Remark that the handkerchiefs cannot stand being apart from one another. Then open the cone to show that the handkerchief has vanished. Have the spectator lift the handkerchief, bringing it into audience view. The audience sees that the vanished handkerchief has apparently re-appeared, tied to the end of the handkerchief held all along by the spectator.

## 45.  They Jumped

The spectator signs his initials on the corner of a handkerchief. He holds this handkerchief in his right hand. The magician signs the corner of another handkerchief and has the spectator hold this handkerchief in his left hand. The two handkerchiefs change places instantly.

METHOD: The principle of concealing one handkerchief inside another is exploited here to bring about a transposition of two handkerchiefs. Required are five or six white 18″ cotton handkerchiefs. Spread one out on a table as shown in Figure 343. Bring end D up to a point above the middle, Figure 344. Turn the handkerchief over, Figure 345. Then bring end B up to the top of the handkerchief, Figure 346.

Grasp the handkerchief at X with the left hand and at Y with the right hand. Bring this portion of the handkerchief over to the position shown in Figure 347. Starting at the bottom, roll the handkerchief over onto itself to form a long cylindrical bundle. Place it on top of another handkerchief in the position indicated in Figure 348.

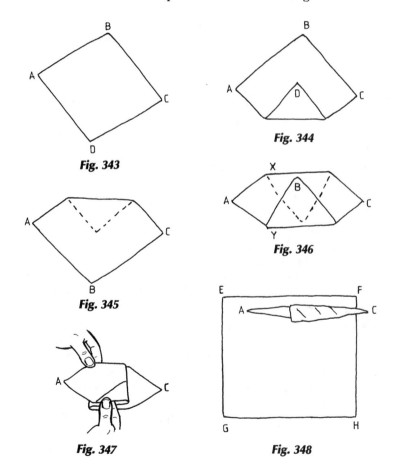

Fig. 343

Fig. 344

Fig. 345

Fig. 346

Fig. 347

Fig. 348

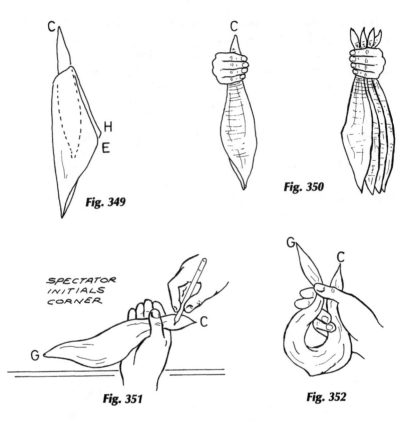

Fig. 349

Fig. 350

SPECTATOR
INITIALS
CORNER

Fig. 351

Fig. 352

Sign your initials at corner F. Then bring corner E down to corner H, Figure 349. The rolled-up handkerchief is now concealed inside the other handkerchief.

Have the prepared handkerchief on the table along with three or four unprepared handkerchiefs. The spectator sits across the table from you.

To present the routine, grasp the prepared handkerchief in the right hand. Hold the other handkerchiefs in the left hand, Figure 350. Hold corner C against the tabletop, Figure 351, and have the spectator sign his initials on this corner with a pencil.

With the left hand, bring corner G into the right hand so it is higher than corner C, Figure 352. Place the right hand under the table and have the spectator grasp the handkerchief by the corner. Since corner G is closest to the spectator, he will grasp the handkerchief by this corner.

Release your grip on corner G but hold firmly to corner C. As you draw the right hand back, you will pull the rolled-up handkerchief out of the handkerchief held by the spectator. Pretend to initial the corner of this handkerchief, then bring it under the table and ask the spectator to hold it in his left hand.

Remind the spectator that he initialed a handkerchief using his right hand, and that he holds this handkerchief in his right hand. Command the two handkerchiefs to change places. The spectator brings the handkerchiefs up onto the table and discovers that the handkerchief with his initials is now in his left hand.

Another presentation is to have the spectator hold in his right hand the handkerchief he thinks has his initials. Pretend to initial the corner of another handkerchief. Instead of placing this handkerchief in the spectator's left hand, hold it in your right hand. Command a transposition. Then bring your handkerchief into view to show that it has the spectator's initials. The spectator's handkerchief has your initials. In this version the initials changed places.

## 46.  Twentieth-Century Silks

This is Lyle Laughlin's streamlined approach to the classic trick in which two handkerchiefs are knotted together and placed in a container. Another handkerchief is vanished, only to reappear between the other two handkerchiefs.

Four handkerchiefs are used. Prepare two handkerchiefs as indicated in "Come Back Silk" (No. 44), Figures 334–340. Hold this handkerchief in the right hand and an unprepared handkerchief in the left hand, Figure 341. Knot the ends together, Figure 353. Then tuck the handkerchiefs into a hat or cardboard box. The prepared handkerchief goes in first. The situation is shown in Figure 354.

Pick up the remaining handkerchief. Tuck it into the "Impromptu Vanisher" (No. 28). Tap the newspaper cone against the table. Then open it to show the handkerchief has vanished.

Curl the left hand around the corner of the handkerchief that protrudes from the top of the box. The right hand pulls the handkerchief upward, Figure 355.

Continue pulling upward in a smooth motion, allowing the prepared handkerchief to unfurl as it is pulled from the box. The result is that you will pull out three handkerchiefs tied together in a chain. From the audience's view, it appears as though the vanished handkerchief ended up tied between the other two handkerchiefs.

Fig. 353

Fig. 354

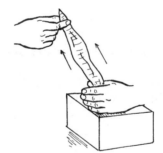

Fig. 355

# CUT AND RESTORED

Effects with handkerchiefs cut and restored first appeared in one of the rarest magic books, *Sports and Pastimes* (1676). Although the literature on this effect is small, some of the most ingenious tricks in magic are those where a handkerchief is cut and magically restored.

## 47. Decapitated Knot

The end of a paper napkin is knotted. The magician then cuts the knot off. Immediately the knot is restored onto the napkin. Only one napkin is used. The knot is actually separated from the napkin, yet at the finish the napkin can be passed for inspection. This routine is based on a brilliant trick of Fred Culpitt's.

METHOD: Paper napkins are used in this routine because one must be cut (and therefore destroyed) as part of the preparation. The trick works as well with handkerchiefs.

Full-size table napkins are usually folded in quarters. This would be too bulky for our purposes, so we will begin by arranging the napkin into just two layers, Figure 356. Then bunch it up a bit, Figure 357. This makes it easier to tie a knot in the napkin. Tie a knot at end B, then cut this knot off, Figure 358.

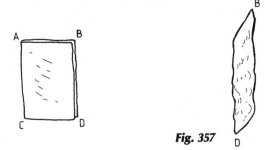

**Fig. 356**

**Fig. 357**

Open another napkin so it is in just two layers. Bunch it up a bit and tie a knot in one end. Do not tighten the knot. Slip the extra knot into the genuine knot, then tighten the genuine knot, Fig. 359. Have this prepared paper napkin on the table along with four or five unprepared napkins.

To present the trick, pick up an unprepared napkin, open it so it is two layers thick, and tie a knot in the end. Place the knotted napkin on the table alongside the prepared napkin. Pick up another napkin and similarly tie a knot in the end. Place the knotted napkin alongside the first napkin.

Repeat this process with one or two of the remaining napkins. As you do this, remark that you were once at a fancy dinner party where you saw a magician do a remarkable trick with a linen napkin. Not being able to afford linen, you will use rare and expensive paper napkins obtained from a local supermarket. Gather all of the napkins and pretend to look them over. Eventually pick the prepared napkin. Hold it with the right hand as shown in Figure 359. The audience's view is shown in Figure 360.

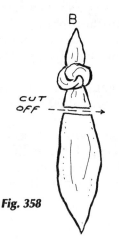

**Fig. 358**

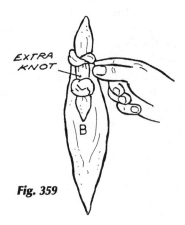

**Fig. 359**

As you turn to the left to get a pair of scissors from the table, slip the left thumb under the extra knot as shown in Figure 361. Pivot this knot upright. At the same time, the left fingers bring the genuine knot down behind the napkin. The situation now is shown in Figure 362-A. In the meantime, the right hand picks up the scissors from the table.

Pretend to cut the knot from the napkin. You actually grasp the extra knot between the scissor blades and work it free of the genuine knot. Once the knot is free, let it fall to the table.

Place the scissors on the table. Pick up the extra knot with the right hand. Display it for a second, then roll it into a ball and place it in the left hand. The back of the left hand is held toward the audience so the spectators do not see that the extra knot is placed against the left third and fourth fingers, Figure 362-B. These two fingers curl in and hold the extra knot in place.

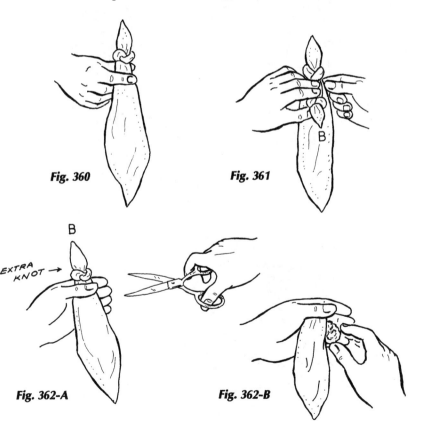

Fig. 360          Fig. 361

B

EXTRA KNOT →

Fig. 362-A          Fig. 362-B

The right hand grasps the napkin with the fingers on top, thumb below, Figure 362-C, and pivots it upright, Figure 363. The napkin is then tucked into the handkerchief pocket of the jacket, Figure 364. The extra knot is allowed to fall to the bottom of the pocket. The napkin is tucked in just far enough so it will remain in the pocket when the hands are removed.

Snap the fingers, then remove the napkin. Do this slowly. You do not want the extra knot to be pulled out of the pocket by accident. Show the knotted end apparently restored. The audience will be skeptical. It will assume the knot has simply been stuck back on. Untie the knot (or have a spectator do it) and spread out the napkin to show that it is indeed fully restored.

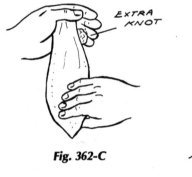

**Fig. 362-C**

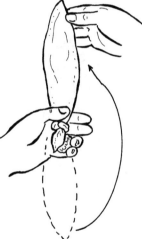

**Fig. 363**

**Fig. 364**

## 48.  Cut Up

Jeanne van Zandt devised a clever way to bring about the effect in which a handkerchief is cut in half and restored. This version uses two handkerchiefs. They are openly placed in a paper tube. The ends of the handkerchiefs protrude from the ends of the tube. A spectator cuts the tube in half. Both handkerchiefs are immediately withdrawn and shown to be unharmed.

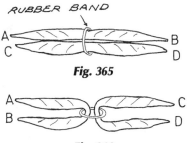

**Fig. 365**

**Fig. 366**

METHOD: Use two 18″ handkerchiefs of the same color. Place them on the table and slip a rubber band over them as shown in Figure 365. The rubber band should be of a size to fit snugly, but not too tightly.

Rearrange the handkerchiefs by bringing end B to the left and end C to the right, Figure 366. This completes the preparation. The handkerchiefs, arranged as shown in Figure 366, are placed on the table until the time of performance.

In addition to the prepared handkerchiefs, you will need an 8½″ by 11″ piece of paper, some transparent tape and a pair of scissors. Fold the paper into thirds, then straighten it out.

To perform the trick, display the handkerchiefs as shown in Figure 367. The performer's view is given in Figure 368. Grasp the paper at the top between the left forefinger and middle finger, Figure 369.

Bring the right hand up behind the paper and deposit the handkerchiefs between the left thumb and first finger, Figure 370. The right hand then folds the right third of the paper over the handkerchiefs, Figure 371. The left hand folds the left third of the paper over to the right, forming a paper tube with the handkerchiefs inside. Use transparent tape to keep the tube from opening.

Grasp the protruding ends of the handkerchiefs and pull them

**Fig. 367**

**Fig. 368**

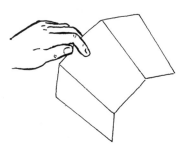

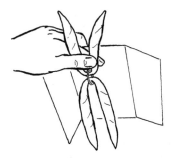

**Fig. 369**

**Fig. 370**

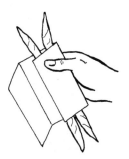

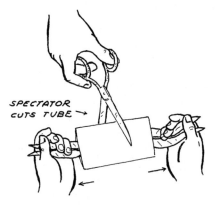

**Fig. 371**

SPECTATOR
CUTS TUBE →

**Fig. 372**

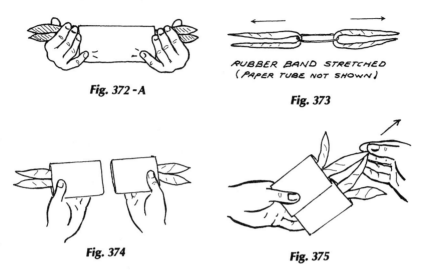

Fig. 372 -A

RUBBER BAND STRETCHED
(PAPER TUBE NOT SHOWN)

Fig. 373

Fig. 374

Fig. 375

slightly apart. Push the tube against the palms with the little finger, Figure 372-A, to keep the tube in place when it is cut. The spectator cuts through the center of the tube as shown in Figure 372. By pulling the ends of the handkerchief, you are pulling the centers apart, as shown in the exposed view of Figure 373. The spectator cuts through the rubber band, not the handkerchiefs.

When the spectator has cut through the tube completely, move the hands in so they grasp the halves of the tube as shown in Figure 374. Then bring the two halves together as indicated in Figure 375. Grasp one end of each handkerchief between the right thumb and first finger, Figure 375. Pull the handkerchiefs out to show them fully restored.

If performed as a platform trick, use brightly colored construction paper to make the tube.

## 49.  Ultra Cut

In this remarkable trick a handkerchief is actually cut in half. The handkerchief is immediately restored. Only one handkerchief is used. There are no gimmicks.

The principle behind this trick appeared in a 1943 issue of *The Phoenix*, a magic magazine. The trick did not attract widespread attention until the magician Phoa Yan Tiong developed a brilliant

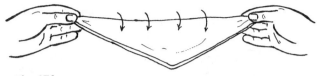

**Fig. 376**

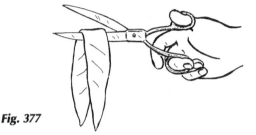

**Fig. 377**

handling. The following routine is based on Phoa's version of the trick.

METHOD: The restoration of the handkerchief is only apparent. You will destroy a handkerchief each time the trick is performed. For this reason you may wish to practice with paper napkins or inexpensive cloth handkerchiefs. If you use a napkin, there are slight changes in the handling that should be obvious. For example, in Figure 376 you cannot twist the napkin. Rather, you will have to place it on the table and roll it ropewise. Otherwise the handling is nearly identical to that described here.

Use an 18″ handkerchief or larger. The trick can be done close up or as a platform trick, and you can be completely surrounded by your audience.

Hold the handkerchief by diagonally opposite corners. Twirl it toward you in the direction shown by the arrows in Figure 376. When the handkerchief has been twisted ropewise, place its center on the lower blade of a pair of scissors, Figure 377. While the left hand grasps the ends of the handkerchief, the right hand cuts the handkerchief in half.

The cut is made exactly at the center, as shown by the dotted lines in Figure 378. The result of the cut is shown in Figure 379. Put the scissors down. Display one half of the handkerchief in each hand. Say, "It looks as if the handkerchief has been cut in half. That's what is known as an optical illusion."

Place the right half of the handkerchief on the table. Grasp the other half in the hands, Figure 380. Separate corner A from corner B and move corner A over to the left, Figure 381.

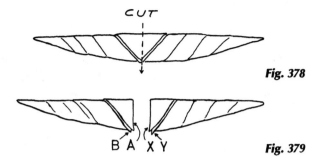

*Fig. 378*

*Fig. 379*

Hold this portion of the handkerchief in the left hand in the position shown in Figure 381. Pick up the other half of the handkerchief. Hold it in the right hand, oriented as in Figure 382. Fold corner X over to the right, Figure 383.

Place this portion of the handkerchief on top of the other portion, Figure 384. It is important that this portion be slightly lower than the other. Thus, corners X and Y are lower than A and B.

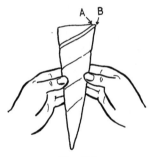

*Fig. 380*

*Fig. 381*

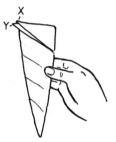

*Fig. 382*

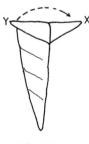

*Fig. 383*

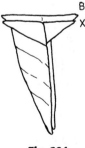

*Fig. 384*

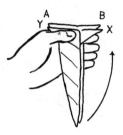

*Fig. 385*

*Fig. 386*

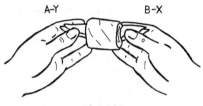

*Fig. 387*

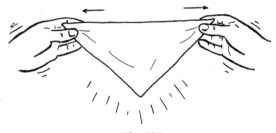

*Fig. 388*

*Fig. 389*

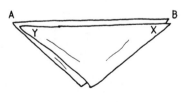

*Fig. 390*

Bring the lower ends up in the direction indicated by the arrow in Figure 385. Continue bringing these ends up and over the top, Figure 386. Grasp ends A and Y between the left thumb and first finger. Grasp ends B and X between the right thumb and first finger. Make sure the thumbs conceal the ends from audience view. The situation is shown in Figure 387.

Draw the hands apart. The handkerchief will unfurl and fall to the position shown in Figure 388. From the audience's view, the handkerchief has been restored.

To reinforce the illusion, holding the handkerchief as in Figure 388, twirl it rope fashion as in Figure 376. Bring the ends together in the left hand. Then tug on the center with the right first finger, Figure 389. Say, "As you can see, the handkerchief was never cut. It was all an illusion."

The true situation, unknown to the audience, is that the handkerchief is still in two pieces, Figure 390. The reason for placing the X-Y portion of the handkerchief slightly below the A-B portion, shown in Figure 384, is to insure that when you reach the position of Figure 390, the X-Y portion will be concealed behind the A-B portion. This means that the cut edges will not be apparent to the audience.

Once mastered, this is an exceptional visual illusion.

# PRODUCTIONS

Perhaps the effect that most surprises audiences is the one in which a solid object is produced seemingly from nowhere. The secrets explained in this chapter allow you to produce everything from magic wands to large bottles of soda. Some of the tricks, like the "Bottle Production" (No. 51), are nearly impromptu. Others, like "Double Appear" (No. 52), can be set up in just a few minutes to produce spectacular effects.

## 50.  Produce a Wand

A handkerchief is shown empty and is folded to form an impromptu bag. The magician remarks that when he was a youngster, he did not have much money. With a dollar to his name, he could purchase only a small magic wand. Reaching into the bag he produces a short wand.

Fortunately a small wand works the same as a big wand. The magician waves the small wand over the handkerchief bag. Then he reaches into the bag and produces a solid 12″ wand.

METHOD: The wand can be made from a piece of dowel 12″ long and about ½″ in diameter. It can also be made from a cardboard tube. If the trick is done under strictly impromptu conditions, use a 12″ ruler.

**Fig. 391**

In either case, the apparatus is tucked into the belt on the right side as shown in Figure 391. The ruler should be tucked in for about a third of its length. Put on a jacket. Keep the jacket unbuttoned. The jacket should completely cover the wand.

Use an opaque 27″ handkerchief. In presenting the routine, fold the handkerchief in quarters as described in "The Holdup" (No. 4), but with the open ends on the right instead of the left.

Hold the impromptu handkerchief bag in the right hand. Reach into the nearest compartment with the left hand. This compartment is shown by the arrow in Figure 392.

The left hand slides right through the handkerchief as indicated in Figure 393. As it does, it curls inward, Figure 394, slips inside the jacket and takes the wand out of the belt. The wand is drawn inside the handkerchief. It is held at the top by the right hand. The performer's view is shown in Figure 395.

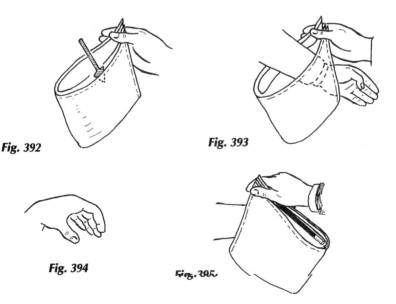

**Fig. 392**

**Fig. 393**

**Fig. 394**

**Fig. 395**

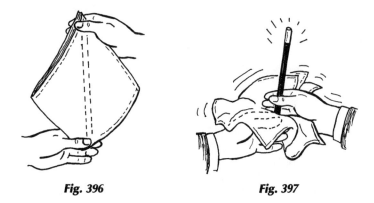

**Fig. 396**                    **Fig. 397**

Remark that as a youngster you had only a dollar. Even then a dollar did not go very far. All it bought was a small wand. Pretend to remove a small wand from inside the handkerchief bag with the left hand. The hand is actually empty.

Say, "It worked its magic anyway." Wave the invisible wand over the handkerchief bag. The left hand then grasps the wand or ruler through the cloth at the bottom of the handkerchief bag as shown in Figure 396. Then the right hand slides the handkerchief downward to reveal the wand, Figure 397.

If the wand is a hollow tube, you can fill it with small silks, ribbon or rope. After the wand is loaded into the handkerchief bag, the small silks are produced by pulling them out of the open top of the wand. Then the wand itself is produced. Note that in Figure 393 the left hand can reach into the jacket's right sleeve to steal a parcel of rolled-up silks, another wand, or any small object that can be concealed in the sleeve. It is also possible to steal small objects concealed inside the shirt.

### 51.  Bottle Production

A handkerchief is shown empty and placed over the right hand. The magician snaps his fingers, then brings his right hand out from under the handkerchief to show that he has produced a half dollar.

"About all a half dollar will buy these days," he says, pausing for dramatic emphasis, "is a bottle of soda." He reaches under the handkerchief and produces a *large* bottle of soda!

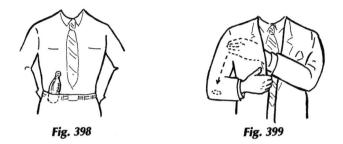

**Fig. 398**                    **Fig. 399**

METHOD: The bottle production is based on a startling trick of Bob Read's. It can be done as a close-up trick or as part of a platform routine. It is one of the best of all production tricks and it is accomplished without gimmicks or elaborate preparation.

The bottle is tucked inside the trousers on the right side for about a third of its length. The neck is angled over to the left. The position of the bottle with the jacket removed is shown in the exposed view of Figure 398. This method of concealment was suggested by U. F. Grant for the production of a bottle from a newspaper.

Fold a 27″ handkerchief up and place it in the inside left jacket pocket. Place a half dollar in the inside right jacket pocket. This completes the preparation.

To present the trick, reach into the inside right jacket pocket with the left hand, Figure 399. Take the half dollar out of the pocket and drop it down the right jacket sleeve. Keep the right hand bent at the elbow so the coin will not fall past the elbow. In Figure 399 the jacket is unbuttoned, and the jacket conceals the bottle from audience view.

Bring the left hand into view. Act puzzled that the item you wanted was not where you thought it was. Then reach into the inside left jacket pocket with the right hand and withdraw the handkerchief. Keep the right arm bent at the elbow so the coin remains in place.

Unfold the handkerchief and show it on both sides. Then clip the center of the handkerchief between the left thumb and first finger. Drop the right hand down behind the handkerchief as you prepare to place the right hand under the handkerchief. As the right hand is lowered, allow the coin to slide out of the sleeve, Figure 400. Catch the coin in the right hand.

Bring the right hand up under the center of the handkerchief. Show the left hand empty. Then regrip the handkerchief as shown in Figure 401, with the left thumb and first finger on the near side, the other fingers on the far side. Grasp the coin through the handkerchief

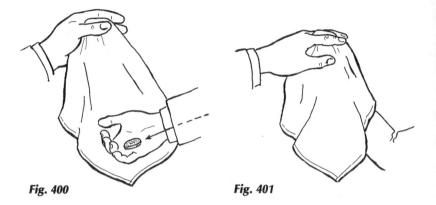

**Fig. 400**                    **Fig. 401**

with the left hand. Say, "I forgot to show you my right hand." Bring out the right hand to show it empty, Figure 402. The handkerchief is held at about chest level. Thus the left hand is at the same level as the neck of the bottle.

Say, "In the old days, magicians produced all sorts of things. Nowadays, this is just about all I can afford." Bring the right hand under the handkerchief. Turn from the waist to the right. As you do, bring the right hand out into view. Raise it to a point above eye level. Look at the coin as if amazed at the production.

As the right hand moves to the right, it will pull at the jacket, causing it to open. Bend forward a bit and raise the right hip. At the same time force the abdomen out. This makes the bottle tilt forward away from the body, making it easy for you to grasp the neck with the left thumb and first finger. An exposed view, with the handkerchief removed, is shown in Figure 403.

As you turn back to face front, ease the body away from the stationary left hand. This movement, combined with the above action, causes the bottle to slide free of the trousers. Figure 404 is an exposed view. Figure 405 is a view as seen by the audience.

Drop the coin into a glass on the table. Say, "And all you can buy with fifty cents these days is this." The right hand, palm up, goes under the handkerchief. Allow the base of the bottle to rest on the right palm. Then lift the handkerchief to reveal the bottle, Figure 406.

Drop the handkerchief on the table. Slap the side of the bottle with the left hand to emphasize that it is a solid bottle.

Instead of producing a coin, you can merely pantomime the action, or you can produce a small wand that you have tucked under the band of the wristwatch. The watch is on the right wrist. Show the right hand empty, then place it under the handkerchief.

The left hand grasps the handkerchief as in Figure 401. The left thumb and first finger grasp the wand through the handkerchief. Pull the right hand back far enough to cause the wand to slide free of the watch. Then grasp the wand with the right hand and bring the right hand into view.

Fig. 402

Fig. 403

Fig. 404

Fig. 405

Fig. 406

Another alternative is to produce a small flashlight in the same manner. In this case remark that you wanted to produce a lighted candle to go with wine after dinner. All you could afford was a flashlight. Produce the flashlight, then add, ". . . and a bottle of soda." Produce the bottle of soda for the surprise finish.

## 52.  Rainbow Silks

A blue silk is displayed. The magician strokes this silk and instantly a white silk appears. As the two silks are stroked, a red silk materializes. Finally, a yellow silk appears.

This beautiful barehanded silk production was invented by Frank Chapman. The following method, requiring no apparatus, was developed by Howard Wurst.

METHOD: Required are blue, white, red and yellow 18″ silk handkerchiefs. The blue silk does not enter into the preparation.

Place one corner of the white silk against a pencil as shown in Figure 407. Hold the end in place with the left thumb. Then wind the silk around the pencil in the direction shown by the arrows in Figure 408. Make sure the winding is done to form a tight, compact bundle.

When you reach the last ½″ of the white silk, hold it in place with the left thumb while the right hand is used to twist the end of the white silk together with one end of the red silk, Figure 409. Twist the ends two or three times. The exact number of twists can be determined by trial and error.

Hold the twisted corners in place with the left thumb. The right hand then winds the red silk around the pencil in the same way as was done with the white silk, Figure 409-A.

When you reach the last ½″ of the red silk, twist this corner around a corner of the yellow silk. Then wind the yellow silk around the pencil in the direction of the arrows in Figure 409-A. Wind the silk so it forms a tight, compact bundle.

Slide the bundle off the end of the pencil, Figure 410. The bundle of three silks should be about 2″–3″ long. Use the point of the pencil to tuck end X of the yellow silk into the bundle as shown in Figure 410. This completes the preparation.

The bundle can be placed on the table near the blue silk. When ready to perform the routine, grasp one end of the blue silk with the left hand. The right hand grasps the bundle of three silks and holds it

**Fig. 407**

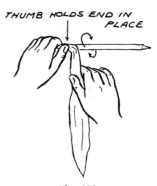

THUMB HOLDS END IN PLACE

**Fig. 408**

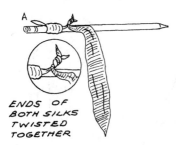

ENDS OF BOTH SILKS TWISTED TOGETHER

**Fig. 409**

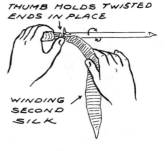

THUMB HOLDS TWISTED ENDS IN PLACE

WINDING SECOND SILK

**Fig. 409-A**

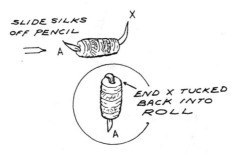

SLIDE SILKS OFF PENCIL

END X TUCKED BACK INTO ROLL

**Fig. 410**

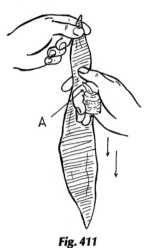

**Fig. 411**

**Fig. 412**

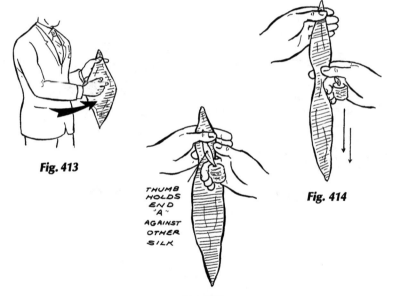

**Fig. 413**

**Fig. 414**

**Fig. 415**

in the loosely curled right second, third and fourth fingers with end A uppermost. The end of the blue silk is then gripped between the right thumb and forefinger as shown in Figure 411.

If you are working away from the table, another approach is this. Place the bundle of three silks into the right jacket pocket. Remove the blue silk from the left jacket pocket with the left hand. Turn so the left side is toward the audience. Snap the blue silk in the air to show that it is unprepared. At the same time, place the right hand in the pocket and grasp the bundle of three silks between the right second, third and fourth fingers. End A of the bundle is uppermost. The position of the body at this point is shown in Figure 412.

Bring the left hand in closer to the body. At the same time, bring the right hand out of the pocket. The bundle of three silks is gripped by the loosely curled fingers. Then bring the right hand behind the blue silk, Figure 413. The right hand is thus hidden from audience view as it moves out of the pocket and behind the blue silk.

Lower the blue silk so the upper corner can be clipped between the right thumb and first finger. Turn so the right side is toward the audience. The blue silk runs over the backs of the right second, third and fourth fingers as shown in Figure 411. The blue silk plus the right fingers screen the concealed bundle from audience view.

Slide the right hand down the blue silk, Figure 414. When the right hand slides off the lower end of the blue silk, bring the right hand back up to the left hand. Slip the protruding corner A of the white silk under the left thumb, Figure 415. Immediately slide the right hand downward again. Since end A is held in place, the white silk will unwind from inside the bundle. The effect is that the white silk materializes from nowhere.

Display the two silks. Then produce the red silk in the same way. Finally produce the yellow silk in the same way. All attention should be directed to the silks in the left hand. Do not look at the right hand. As the right hand slides down the silks, raise the left hand so it is above shoulder level. Follow the movement of the left hand with the eyes. This keeps audience attention away from the right hand.

Most silk productions require boxes or other special apparatus to bring about the production. "Rainbow Silks" is a barehanded production which, if performed to graceful music, is a striking and memorable visual routine.

## 53.  Double Appear

The magician displays a blue silk handkerchief. He snaps it in the air. Instantly, a red silk appears tied to the end of the blue silk. The magician blows on the knot, making it dissolve.

He snaps the red silk in the air. Instantly, a yellow silk appears tied to the end of the red silk. The magician blows on the knot, making it dissolve. The three silks may now be used in subsequent tricks.

This elegant routine was developed by Eric C. Lewis and Harold Rice.

METHOD: The routine uses three ordinary 18″ silk handkerchiefs. There are no gimmicks. The handkerchiefs are blue, red and yellow. Tie the red silk to the yellow silk with a square knot. Upset the knot as described in "The Square Knot" (No. 32). Then slide the knot toward the end of the silk, Figure 416. Later on you will blow on this knot and simultaneously pull the silks in opposite directions, causing the knot to dissolve.

Place the knotted silks out flat on the table, Figure 417. Fold the yellow silk in half along the dotted line shown in Figure 417, bringing end D up in the direction of the arrow to meet end B. The result is shown in Figure 418.

**Fig. 416**

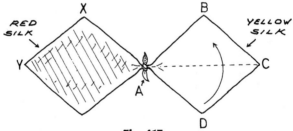

**Fig. 417**

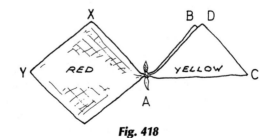

**Fig. 418**

Roll ends B and D downward so the yellow silk is in the ropelike shape shown in Figure 419. Fold about 2″ of end C up at right angles to the yellow silk, Figure 420. The exact length of this portion is determined by the thickness of the final bundle, but 2″ should be about right.

Beginning at the far right, roll the yellow silk toward the left, Figure 421, until it touches end A. Make the roll snug and neat. Bring end C down in back of the bundle, Figure 422. Then bring end C up

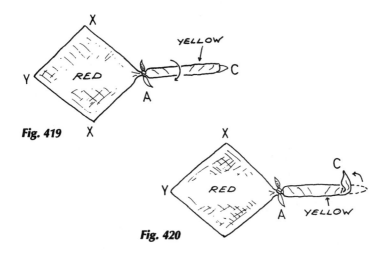

**Fig. 419**

**Fig. 420**

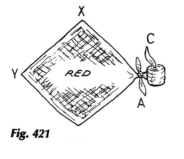

**Fig. 421**

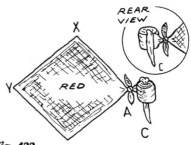

**Fig. 422**

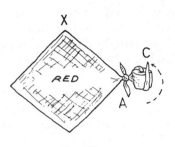

Fig. 423

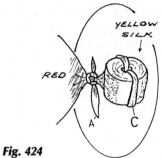

Fig. 424

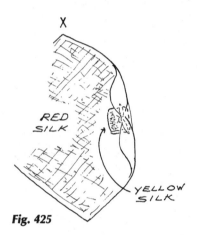

Fig. 425

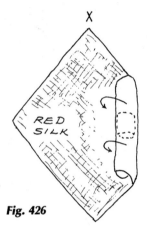

Fig. 426

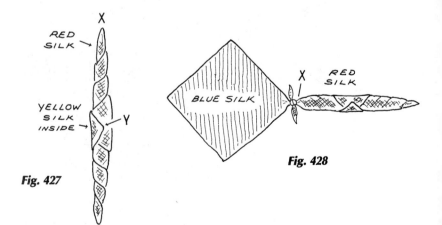

Fig. 427

Fig. 428

in front, Figure 423. Make sure end C is wrapped snugly around the bundle. Tuck end C into the center of the bundle using the blunt end of a toothpick. In Figure 423, note that end C should be no more than ¼″–½″. If it is longer, it will hold the bundle too securely, making it difficult later to release the rolled-up silk. After end C has been tucked in, the bundle will look as it does in Figure 424.

At the corner where the red silk is knotted to the yellow silk, the red silk will be pleated or gathered to form a shell-like pocket. If it does not show on the upper side, turn the apparatus over to bring this gently curved pocket uppermost. Place the rolled-up yellow silk into this pleat, Figure 425.

Roll the red silk over to the left, Figure 426. The finished product is shown in Figure 427. The red silk can be held by corner X and displayed. The folds of the red silk will keep it from unrolling.

Place the rolled-up red silk on the table alongside the blue silk. Tie corner X of the red silk to one corner of the blue silk, Figure 428. Use the square knot and upset the knot as before.

Now roll the red silk to the left using the procedure shown in Figures 420–427. This completes the preparation.

To present the trick, pick up the blue silk by corner X and display the silk. Grasp corner Y with the other hand. Release corner X and simultaneously snap the blue silk in the air. The red silk will instantly appear, knotted to the end of the blue silk, Figure 429.

Grasp one handkerchief in each hand. The hands should be close to the knot, Figure 430. Bring the knotted corners to the lips. Blow on the silks. At the same time, gently tug them apart. The knot dissolves.

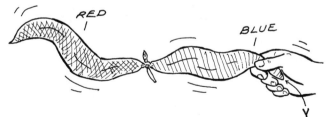

**Fig. 429**

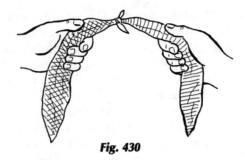

**Fig. 430**

Place the blue silk aside. Grasp the red silk by corner X, display the silk for a second, then grasp it by corner Y with the other hand. Release corner X. Simultaneously snap the red silk, and the yellow silk will instantly appear, tied to a corner of the red silk. Bring the knotted corners to your lips, blow on the silks and gently tug on them to make the knot dissolve.

The three silks are now unprepared and ordinary, and may be used for further tricks.

# ANIMATION

Handkerchief magic is perhaps unique in the sense that one can use the apparatus itself to form amusing creatures that seem to spring to life. Three of the best such handkerchief figures are described in this chapter. Some, like "Fatima" (No. 54), produce amusing visual effects. Others, like "The Rabbit" (No. 56), perform magic tricks. The folds in this chapter can be routined together. For an encore, you can perform "The Mouse" (No. 31).

## 54. Fatima

Fatima is one of the simplest figures that can be made with a handkerchief. It does a dance, then kicks its leg.

Use a 27" handkerchief. Form a knot midway between corners A and B, Figure 431.

Grasp corners C and D, Figure 432. Twirl the handkerchief in the direction shown by the arrow, Figure 433. Continue doing this until the handkerchief is taut. The result is shown in Figure 434.

Stand the figure upright. Hold it at the top, near the "head," with the right hand, and at the bottom with the left hand as shown in Figure 435.

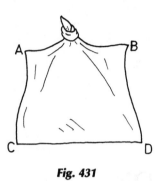

Fig. 431

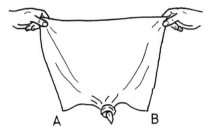

Fig. 432

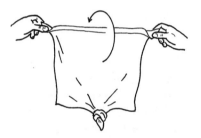

Fig. 433

Fig. 434

Fig. 435

Fig. 436

By moving the left fingers back and forth, you can animate the figure, making the legs move as if the figure is dancing. Once this movement is established, begin moving the head from side to side with the right hand. The result is an amusing animated figure.

To finish, release one leg. It will kick upward as shown in Figure 436. To insure that the leg will kick sharply, when you release it from the left hand, simultaneously flick it upward with the right little finger. Make sure that the leg is under tension just before you release it.

William Larsen, Sr., suggested a routine of simple tricks with the handkerchief, after which he would say, "Many of you wonder how I accomplish these things. Actually, I have an invisible assistant, Fatima. Hers is the power that permits miracles." After Fatima has been constructed, Larsen recited the following verse as the figure became animated:

> Fatima was a dancer gay.
> For fifty cents she'd dance this way.
> But if one dollar you would pay,
> She'd do the ta ra ra boom de aye.

As the last line of the stanza is recited, one leg of the figure is released to perform the kick of Figure 436.

## 55.  Willie

This is a quick, simple handkerchief fold that produces mouselike (or catlike) ears. Begin by placing an 18″ handkerchief flat on the table, Figure 437. Fold the sides in to the center, Figure 438.

Grasp the handkerchief at the sides as indicated in Figure 438 and lift it off the table. The handkerchief will fold in half, Figure 439.

Place the folded handkerchief on the table, Figure 440. Grasp corners A and C with the left hand, corners B and D with the right hand, Figure 441. Pull the corners in opposite directions, the left hand moving to the left, the right hand to the right.

The result is a set of ears that you can place on your head or on a child's head, Figure 442.

You can also make a hand puppet with the same fold. After you have grasped the corners as in Figure 441 and pulled in opposite

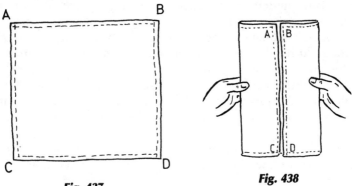

**Fig. 437**

**Fig. 438**

**Fig. 439**

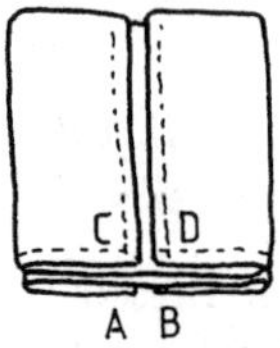

**Fig. 440**

**Fig. 441**

**Fig. 442**

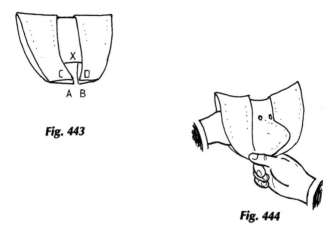

**Fig. 443**

**Fig. 444**

directions, bring the corners together as shown in Figure 443. Hold the corners in place with the right hand. The edge of the handkerchief, shown as X in Figure 443, is clipped between the left thumb and first finger. This forms a nose. The puppet looks as shown in Figure 444. The eyes are drawn with a pencil.

By wiggling the left thumb you can make the nose move. Have the puppet face the audience. Say, "This is my friend Willie. He's going to sing 'Row, Row, Row Your Boat' . . . in Latin." Have the puppet slowly turn and look up at you. Then you say, "I mean, he's going to *hum* 'Row, Row, Row Your Boat' in Latin." Have the puppet face front again. Hum the tune as you animate the puppet.

A handkerchief figure like Willie can be used in conjunction with other tricks. For example, if you perform "Matchmaker" (No. 38), you can pretend that the necessary information as to the color chosen by the spectator is coming to you by way of your telepathic friend Willie.

## 56.  The Rabbit

Magicians are expected to produce a rabbit. If you know how to make a rabbit from a handkerchief, you will always have on hand a creature who can assist in performing magic tricks.

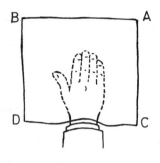

*Fig. 445-A*

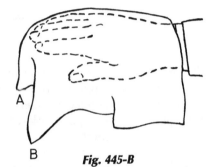

*Fig. 445-B*

*Fig. 446*

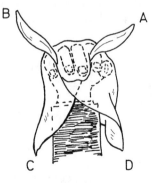

*Fig. 447*

D C

**Fig. 448**          **Fig. 449**

Place an 18″ white cotton handkerchief over the right hand as shown in Figure 445-A. Lift the hand so the handkerchief drapes over the hand as shown in Figure 445-B. The handkerchief should overhang the fingertips by two or three inches. Bend the fingers, Figure 446.

The left hand grasps end A and draws it up between the right first and second fingers. The left hand then draws end B up between the right third and fourth fingers. The result is shown in Figure 447. To complete the formation of the rabbit, pull the lower ends C and D closer together. The finished rabbit is shown in Figure 448.

With just a bit of practice, you can form the rabbit quickly from a handkerchief or table napkin. It should be done out of audience view with the handkerchief held just below the level of the tabletop. Then bring the rabbit up into view as shown in Figure 449.

You can make the rabbit's ears wiggle by moving the fingers. The rabbit can be made to nod and shake its head in a lifelike way. If you have a pocket on the left side of the jacket or shirt, you can make the rabbit look down into the pocket as if searching for food. Since the rabbit is made from a cotton handkerchief, you can remark that its nickname is Peter Cottontail. "Cabbage" and "lettuce" are slang terms for dollar bills, perhaps because they share a similar color. You can roll up a dollar bill, leave it on the table, then form the rabbit and have it nibble at the bill.

The handkerchief rabbit can even play the part of a magician, as described in the next trick.

## 57.   He Found It!

In this routine, a handkerchief rabbit finds a chosen card. The rabbit even takes a bite out of the chosen card!

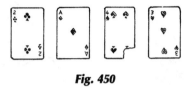

**Fig. 450**

METHOD: Four cards of mixed suits are used. They are the ♣ 2, ◊ A, ♠ 4 and ♡ 3. Tear out the lower right corner of the ♠ 4, Figure 450. Stack the cards in 2-A-4-3 order from the top down. Square up the packet and place it in your card case or wallet.

**Fig. 451**                              **Fig. 452**

To perform the trick, remove the squared packet and hold it face down in the left hand so the torn corner is at the lower left. Spread the cards from left to right between the hands, Figure 451. The faces of the cards are toward the audience as indicated in Figure 452. The torn corner is thus concealed from audience view. Hold the packet, fanned, in the left hand, as shown in Figure 452.

Ask the spectator for a number from one to four. If he names One, spell O-N-E, counting a card for each letter from the spectator's left to his right. Thus, using your right first finger, you would tap the ♣ 2, then the ◊ A, then the ♠ 4 as you spell O-N-E. You end up on the ♠ 4, so this will be the chosen card.

If the spectator names Two, spell T-W-O and count to the chosen card in the same way, ending up on the ♠ 4. If the spectator names Three, count One-Two-Three as you count to the ♠ 4. Finally, if the spectator names Four, say, "Okay, we'll use the Four, in this case the Four of Spades." Using this system, you have forced the spectator to arrive at the ♠ 4.

**Fig. 453**

Jog the ♠ 4 upward as indicated in Figure 453. The torn corner is still concealed from audience view. Ask the spectator to remember the ♠ 4. Then square up the packet. Turn the packet end for end, then place it face up in the left hand. Then turn the left hand palm down and place the packet face down on the table.

Form the handkerchief rabbit as already explained. Pick up the packet of four cards with the left hand. Take care not to expose the torn corner of the ♠ 4. The torn corner will be at the upper right on the ♠ 4. The ♠ 4 is third down in the packet.

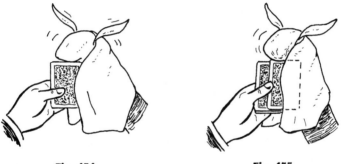

**Fig. 454**                    **Fig. 455**

Bring the rabbit over to the packet and have him nibble at the upper right corner, Figure 454. Then push the top card of the packet (the ♣ 2) into the rabbit's mouth, Figure 455. The rabbit contemplates whether this is the chosen card, decides it is not, and allows this card to fall to the table.

The rabbit takes the next card (the ◊ A) into its mouth, then drops this card on the table. The rabbit takes the next card in its mouth. This card is the chosen card, the ♠ 4. The rabbit nods to indicate that this is the chosen card.

If this handling is followed correctly, the torn corner on the ♠ 4 will be concealed from audience view. The card is taken into the rabbit's mouth in Figure 453 before the card is removed from the packet, so the audience has no chance to spot the torn corner. You still hold the ♡ 3 in the left hand at this point. Place the ♡ 3 on the table.

Grasp the ♠ 4 with the left hand. Pretend the rabbit will not let go. Remark that he must be hungry. Then take the ♠ 4 from the rabbit's mouth to show that he nibbled off a corner of the card—a surprise finish to the trick.

# CARDS AND HANDKERCHIEFS

Many popular tricks go through an evolutionary process whereby one or more difficult sleights are replaced by streamlined handlings. Two of the tricks in this chapter are excellent examples of magical evolution. In both "The Jinx Deck" (No. 58) and "Zombie Card Rise" (No. 60), the reader will find exceptionally strong magic performed with the simplest possible methods. The chapter closes with a trick in which the book you are reading is the major item of apparatus.

## 58. The Jinx Deck

This trick, invented by Martin Gardner, contains a startling twist. A freely shuffled deck of cards is wrapped in a handkerchief. On command, one of the red Aces visibly rises through the cloth. The magician commands the other red Ace to penetrate the handkerchief. Instead, the entire deck drops through the handkerchief! One card remains inside the handkerchief. On inspection it proves to be the chosen card.

Generally, tricks where cards penetrate a handkerchief require advanced sleight of hand. The following method uses no sleights.

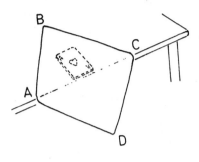

Fig. 456

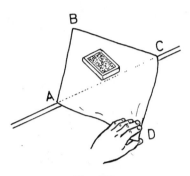

Fig. 457

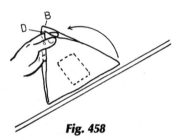

Fig. 458

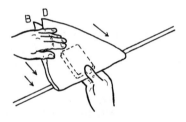

Fig. 459

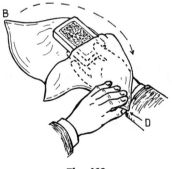

Fig. 460

Fig. 461

METHOD: Beforehand, remove the red Aces and place them face up near the edge of the table. Cover them with a handkerchief as shown in Figure 456.

To present the trick, hand out the deck for shuffling. When the audience is satisfied that the deck is well mixed, take it back and remove the black Aces. Place the Aces face up on the table. Remark that cards sometimes exert a strange sympathetic power over one another. In this case you will demonstrate the effect the black Aces have over the red Aces.

Have the deck given one more shuffle. Then place it face down on the handkerchief, directly over the red Aces, Figure 457. Grasp corner D of the handkerchief with the left hand palm down as shown in Figure 457.

Bring this corner over the deck, Figure 458. The left hand then slides the deck (and the red Aces) off the table onto the waiting right hand, Figure 459. Bring corner D back onto the right arm, Figure 460, to display the deck once more. Tell the audience that the red Aces are somewhere in the deck, but they will try to leave the deck to join the black Aces. You can riffle the front end of the deck with the left fingers as you speak.

Bring corner D of the handkerchief over the deck again. Then grasp the deck with the left hand as shown in Figure 461. This allows the right hand to grip the deck again, as indicated in Figure 462. (This is an exposed view, as seen by the magician. The audience is unaware that the red Aces are outside the handkerchief.)

Use the right first finger to push the Ace upward, making it rise apparently. The audience view is shown in Figure 463. To add drama,

REAR
VIEW →

**Fig. 462**

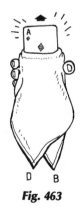

D    B

**Fig. 463**

**Fig. 464**

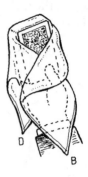

**Fig. 465**

**Fig. 466**

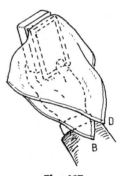

**Fig. 467**

**Fig. 468**

**Fig. 469**

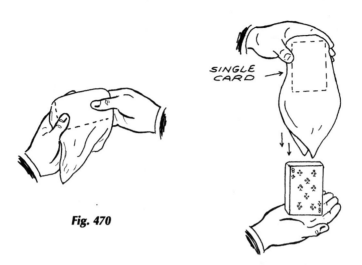

**Fig. 470**

SINGLE CARD →

**Fig. 471**

have the Ace rise about a half-inch. Stop, give the deck a shake, then make the Ace rise full length. Take the Ace with the left hand and place it on the table with the black Aces.

Take the deck at the upper left corner between the left thumb and first finger, Figure 464. This allows the right hand to move under the handkerchief and grasp the deck as shown in Figure 465.

Grasp the corner of the handkerchief at the front of the deck (corner D) with the left hand and lift it to display the deck, Figure 466. Bring corner D back so it lies on the right arm, Figure 467. Riffle the top of the deck with the left fingers as you say, "The other red Ace is in the middle of the deck."

Take corners B and D with the left hand, Figure 468. Bring these corners over the deck. At the same time, turn or tip the right hand so its fingers point to the floor. The position is indicated in Figure 469.

Grasp the deck with the left hand palm up, Figure 470. Remark that you will shake the deck, causing the red Ace to penetrate the handkerchief. Hold the deck in the left hand as shown in Figure 471. Give the handkerchief a shake, then release the deck. Catch it with the right hand as shown in Figure 471. You can fan the deck to emphasize that the entire deck dropped through the handkerchief.

Pause a second. Then say, "That's *almost* the entire deck." Place the deck on the table. Lift the handkerchief to show the other red Ace, Figure 472.

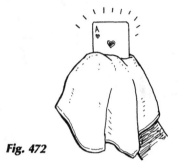

**Fig. 472**

### 59.   Four-Way Prophet

A folded handkerchief is placed on the table. The magician explains that it contains a special set of cards he carries with him whenever he wishes to make a prediction. Two of the cards, the magician explains, will invariably turn face up to predict a chosen card correctly.

To test the claim, he places two packs of cards on the table. One pack is red-backed and the other blue-backed. A spectator deals the red-backed deck into four heaps. He can stop the deal at any time.

The spectator chooses one heap and discards the others. The face card of the chosen heap might be the ♡ A. The handkerchief is unfolded. It contains four cards and two are face up. Their values are added together to arrive, for example, at the number 14.

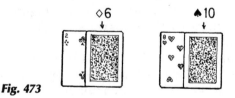

**Fig. 473**

The spectator counts to the fourteenth card in the blue-backed deck. This card is the ♡ A, exactly matching the spectator's chosen card.

METHOD: At work here is a four-way force. The prediction cards are the ♣ 2, ◊ 6, ♡ 8 and ♠ 10. Arrange them in face-to-face pairs as shown in Figure 473.

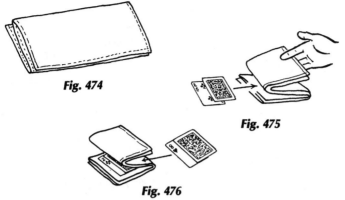

Fig. 474

Fig. 475

Fig. 476

Fold an 18″ handkerchief in thirds as shown in Figure 474. Then fold it in thirds the other way, Figure 475. Place the 2-6 pair in the fold shown by the arrow in Figure 475. Place the 8-10 pair in the other fold as shown by the arrow in Figure 476. The folded handkerchief with the four prediction cards can be carried in the pocket until you are ready to perform.

Arrange a red-backed deck with the ♡ A on top, followed by the ♣ A, ♢ A, ♠ A, in that order. Arrange a blue-backed deck so the ♡ A is 10th from the top, the ♣ A 12th, the ♢ A 14th and the ♠ A 16th.

To present the trick, remove the prefolded handkerchief from the pocket. Place in on the table aligned as in Figure 476. Explain that it contains four cards trained to see the future. Say that two of the cards are face up and that you will add their values to arrive at a card in the blue-backed deck. Note that you have given out all of the pertinent information at the very beginning of the trick.

Hand the spectator the red-backed deck. Have him deal cards off the top one at a time in a row on the table to form four heaps. After he has dealt seven or eight cards, remark that he can stop dealing whenever he chooses. Unknown to him, the bottom card of each heap is an Ace. Since you know the original order of the Aces, you know which Ace is at the bottom of which heap.

After he has dealt four heaps, have him choose one. By noting the position of this heap in the row, you know which Ace is at the bottom. If he chose the first heap, the ♡ A would be at the bottom. If he chose the second heap the ♣ A would be at the bottom, and so on. Assume he chose the first heap. It has the ♡ A at the bottom. You know the ♡ A is 10th down from the top of the blue-backed deck.

Gather the other heaps one on top of the next, give the deck a straight cut and put it aside. To show that the prediction cards total 10,

Fig. 477

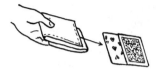

Fig. 478

Fig. 479                    Fig. 480

grasp the handkerchief by the right side and allow the first pair to slide out onto the table, Figure 477. Then change hands. Holding the hankerchief at the left side, allow the other pair to slide out, Figure 478. If the alignment of the handkerchief was correct when you removed it from the pocket, the face-up cards will be the ♣ 2 and ♡ 8. Adding their values produces a total of 10.

Have the spectator count to the 10th card from the top of the blue-backed deck. It will be the ♡ A, correctly matching the face card of the red-backed heap chosen by the spectator.

If the spectator chose the heap with the ♣ A at the face, you know that the matching ♣ A in the blue-backed deck is 12th from the top. To arrive at the number 12, slide the first pair out as shown in Figure 477. Shake the handkerchief a bit more, as though expecting the other cards to slide out. Then grasp the handkerchief with both hands, Figure 479, and flip it over into the left hand, Figure 480.

Slide the second pair out to the left as in Figure 477. The face-up cards will be the ♣ 2 and ♠ 10. Their sum is the number 12. Count to the 12th card in the blue-backed deck and you will arrive at the ♣ A.

If the spectator chooses the heap with the ◊ A at its face, you want to produce a total of 14. To do this, begin by grasping the handkerchief at the left side and sliding out a pair as shown in Figure 478. Then flip the handkerchief over as shown in Figure 480. Slide out the other pair, Figure 478. The two face-up cards will be the ◊ 6 and ♡ 8. When their values are added together, the total will be 14.

If the spectator chooses the heap with the ♠ A at its face, you want to arrive at a total of 16. Start with the handkerchief as in Figure 476.

Pick up the handkerchief and flip it over as shown in Figure 480. Then slide out the first pair, Figure 477, and the second pair, Figure 478. The face-up cards will be the ♠ 10 and ◊ 6. Their total will be 16.

When shaking the cards out of the handkerchief, take care not to turn them over accidentally.

## 60.  Zombie Card Rise

To Eddie Ward goes credit for one of the best impromptu methods of making a chosen card rise out of the deck. As seen by the audience, a deck of cards is covered with a handkerchief. The magician touches the top of the deck with his right first finger. Immediately, one card rises up out of the deck. This proves to be a previously chosen card.

METHOD: Prior to performance, reverse the bottom card of the deck. Place the deck on the table so it extends over the edge about a half-inch, Figure 481. This is so that later the cards can be picked up without fumbling.

**Fig. 481**

To perform the trick, lift off about half the deck. Mix the cards and fan them. Have a spectator remove any card and look at it. Say the card is the ◊ 2.

Have him place the card face down on top of the packet. Then place this packet on the table. Lift up the other half of the deck. This packet has the secretly reversed card on the bottom. Put this packet on top of the other half of the deck. The chosen card is now buried in the middle of the deck.

Cut off about a quarter of the deck from the top and place it on the table. Complete the cut by placing the rest of the deck on top.

Put the deck in the middle of the table and cover it with a spread-out handkerchief. Command the chosen card to turn over. Snap the fingers. Remove the handkerchief. Spread the cards until you come to the reversed card. Cut the deck at this point and complete the cut so the reversed card is on top of the deck.

Ask if this is the chosen card. The spectator will say no. Place this card aside. The chosen card is now on top of the deck.

**Fig. 482**

**Fig. 483**

**Fig. 484**

**Fig. 485**

Hold the deck in the left hand. Cover it with the handkerchief. As you do, use the left thumb to pull the top card down about an inch, Figure 482. This move can be done after the deck is completely covered, thus making it impossible for the audience to see that the top card has been jogged down.

Rub the right first finger against the left jacket sleeve as if to generate static electricity. Then place the first finger against the top of the deck, Figure 483. Lift the first finger. Act disappointed when nothing happens.

Rub the first finger against the sleeve again. Place the first finger against the top of the deck. This time, extend the right little finger and place it against the bottom edge of the jogged card. The position is shown in Figure 484. (The handkerchief has been removed for clarity.)

The little finger bends or curves the protruding card away from the deck. The little finger then slides the protruding card upward where it is trapped between the extended fingers as shown in Figure 485. All of this happens through the handkerchief.

When you failed to make the chosen card reverse itself in the deck, you mentioned that you would try to make it rise out of the pack. Up to this point you have failed. At this point the chosen card is about to rise out of the pack. When it does, act relieved and happy.

As the right hand is raised above the deck, it appears as though the handkerchief is clinging to the first finger, Figure 486. The outline of a playing card can be seen under the handkerchief. When performing the trick, raise the right hand slowly at first. When the card has just cleared the deck, stop for a second, then raise the hand at a quicker pace, as though the card has begun to soar into the air. You can wiggle the right first finger slightly as the card rises.

When the right hand is above the head, grasp it with the left hand and bring the right hand down to chest level. Pinch the card between the right thumb and first finger. Turn the right hand over so the handkerchief falls away from the card. The left hand can be used to aid the process. Display the chosen card as shown in Figure 487.

If you are seated at a table, an added effect can be achieved. Beforehand, spread a napkin out on the lap. Then perform "Zombie Card Rise" up to the point where the chosen card is caught between the right first and fourth fingers, as in Figure 485. The handkerchief should be draped over the deck with the apparatus held so the bottom of the handkerchief is just at the edge of the table.

All attention will be on the chosen card as it begins to rise. This allows you to release the deck so it falls into the lap, Figure 488. Allow the chosen card to rise high in the air. Then have it descend so that the handkerchief is draped over the left hand again.

Bring the hands to the center of the table. Grasp the chosen card through the handkerchief with the right hand, Figure 489. The left hand simultaneously drops to the lap, grips the deck and moves to a position under the center of the table.

Shake the right hand. Allow the chosen card to fall to the table. Flick the handkerchief to show it empty. Then bring the deck up into view. You have thus presented a double effect: The chosen card rose into the air, then the deck penetrated the table.

**Fig. 486**

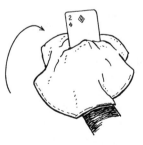

**Fig. 487**

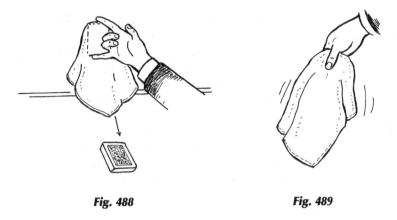

**Fig. 488**                                    **Fig. 489**

## 61.  Magic with "Handkerchief Magic"

The spectator chooses a card from an ordinary deck. The card may be a 10-spot. The spectator opens *Self-Working Handkerchief Magic* to the first page of any chapter and notes the 10th word in the opening sentence. The magician, his back turned, slowly reveals the word chosen by the spectator.

METHOD: There are really two secrets at work here. The first is an ingenious under-the-handkerchief force of a playing card. Have any 10-spot, say the ♠ 10, on top of the deck. Hold the deck face down in the left hand. The right hand picks up an opaque handkerchief and starts to cover the deck.

When the handkerchief is in front of the left hand and therefore screening the deck from audience view, curl the left thumb under the deck, Figure 490, and flip the deck over to a face-up position, Figure 491. Cover the deck so the handkerchief is evenly draped over the left hand as depicted in Figure 492. Note in this drawing that the left thumb lies alongside the deck rather than on top of it. You want the left thumb out of the way so the spectator can freely cut the cards.

Extend the deck to the spectator. Ask him to cut off about half the deck. He lifts a packet of cards through the thickness of the handkerchief, Figure 493.

The left hand is still under the handkerchief. Curl the left thumb under the packet of cards in the left hand and flip over the packet to a face-down position. Then bring the left hand out into view, Figure 494. Thumb off the top card of the packet onto the table, saying, "You cut the deck right here."

**Fig. 490**

**Fig. 491**

**Fig. 492**

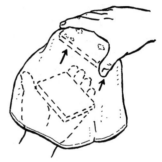

**Fig. 493**

**Fig. 494**

Bring the left hand back under the handkerchief. When the left hand is covered by the handkerchief, curl the left thumb under the packet and flip the packet face up again. Have the spectator replace the cut-off packet on top of the packet in your left hand. To complete the handling, curl the left thumb under the deck and flip the deck over to a face-down position. Remove the handkerchief and place the deck on the table.

The other part of the method has to do with the fact that *Self-Working Handkerchief Magic* has been rigged as a force book. The 10th word of each chapter (and even of the Introduction) is "one." Have the spectator note the value of the card he chose. Have him take this book to a far corner, open it to the first page of any chapter and note the 10th word of the opening sentence. Reveal the word "one" in a dramatic manner.

One way to reveal the word in an amusing way is to use three square cards. Print W on one, O on another, and N on a third. When the spectator has chosen his word, say, "Is this exactly the word you chose?" Display the word as W-O-N, Figure 495. The spectator will reply that you are close but not exactly correct. Next arrange the letters to show Z-O-W (the N turned sideways becomes a Z), Figure 496. Say, "I'm sure the word ZOW isn't in that book." Finally turn the W sideways to produce the word O-N-E as shown in Figure 497.

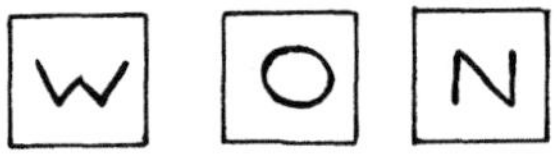

$$\boxed{W}\ \boxed{O}\ \boxed{N}$$

**Fig. 495**

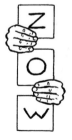

**Fig. 496**

$$\boxed{O}\ \boxed{N}\ \boxed{\text{Ɛ}}$$

**Fig. 497**

A CATALOG OF SELECTED
DOVER BOOKS
IN ALL FIELDS OF INTEREST

# A CATALOG OF SELECTED DOVER
# BOOKS IN ALL FIELDS OF INTEREST

CONCERNING THE SPIRITUAL IN ART, Wassily Kandinsky. Pioneering work by father of abstract art. Thoughts on color theory, nature of art. Analysis of earlier masters. 12 illustrations. 80pp. of text. 5⅜ x 8½. 0-486-23411-8

CELTIC ART: The Methods of Construction, George Bain. Simple geometric techniques for making Celtic interlacements, spirals, Kells-type initials, animals, humans, etc. Over 500 illustrations. 160pp. 9 x 12. (Available in U.S. only.) 0-486-22923-8

AN ATLAS OF ANATOMY FOR ARTISTS, Fritz Schider. Most thorough reference work on art anatomy in the world. Hundreds of illustrations, including selections from works by Vesalius, Leonardo, Goya, Ingres, Michelangelo, others. 593 illustrations. 192pp. 7⅛ x 10¼. 0-486-20241-0

CELTIC HAND STROKE-BY-STROKE (Irish Half-Uncial from "The Book of Kells"): An Arthur Baker Calligraphy Manual, Arthur Baker. Complete guide to creating each letter of the alphabet in distinctive Celtic manner. Covers hand position, strokes, pens, inks, paper, more. Illustrated. 48pp. 8¼ x 11. 0-486-24336-2

EASY ORIGAMI, John Montroll. Charming collection of 32 projects (hat, cup, pelican, piano, swan, many more) specially designed for the novice origami hobbyist. Clearly illustrated easy-to-follow instructions insure that even beginning papercrafters will achieve successful results. 48pp. 8¼ x 11. 0-486-27298-2

BLOOMINGDALE'S ILLUSTRATED 1886 CATALOG: Fashions, Dry Goods and Housewares, Bloomingdale Brothers. Famed merchants' extremely rare catalog depicting about 1,700 products: clothing, housewares, firearms, dry goods, jewelry, more. Invaluable for dating, identifying vintage items. Also, copyright-free graphics for artists, designers. Co-published with Henry Ford Museum & Greenfield Village. 160pp. 8¼ x 11. 0-486-25780-0

THE ART OF WORLDLY WISDOM, Baltasar Gracian. "Think with the few and speak with the many," "Friends are a second existence," and "Be able to forget" are among this 1637 volume's 300 pithy maxims. A perfect source of mental and spiritual refreshment, it can be opened at random and appreciated either in brief or at length. 128pp. 5⅜ x 8½. 0-486-44034-6

JOHNSON'S DICTIONARY: A Modern Selection, Samuel Johnson (E. L. McAdam and George Milne, eds.). This modern version reduces the original 1755 edition's 2,300 pages of definitions and literary examples to a more manageable length, retaining the verbal pleasure and historical curiosity of the original. 480pp. 5⁵⁄₁₆ x 8¼. 0-486-44089-3

ADVENTURES OF HUCKLEBERRY FINN, Mark Twain, Illustrated by E. W. Kemble. A work of eternal richness and complexity, a source of ongoing critical debate, and a literary landmark, Twain's 1885 masterpiece about a barefoot boy's journey of self-discovery has enthralled readers around the world. This handsome clothbound reproduction of the first edition features all 174 of the original black-and-white illustrations. 368pp. 5⅜ x 8½. 0-486-44322-1

STICKLEY CRAFTSMAN FURNITURE CATALOGS, Gustav Stickley and L. & J. G. Stickley. Beautiful, functional furniture in two authentic catalogs from 1910. 594 illustrations, including 277 photos, show settles, rockers, armchairs, reclining chairs, bookcases, desks, tables. 183pp. 6½ x 9¼. 0-486-23838-5

AMERICAN LOCOMOTIVES IN HISTORIC PHOTOGRAPHS: 1858 to 1949, Ron Ziel (ed.). A rare collection of 126 meticulously detailed official photographs, called "builder portraits," of American locomotives that majestically chronicle the rise of steam locomotive power in America. Introduction. Detailed captions. xi+ 129pp. 9 x 12. 0-486-27393-8

AMERICA'S LIGHTHOUSES: An Illustrated History, Francis Ross Holland, Jr. Delightfully written, profusely illustrated fact-filled survey of over 200 American lighthouses since 1716. History, anecdotes, technological advances, more. 240pp. 8 x 10¾. 0-486-25576-X

TOWARDS A NEW ARCHITECTURE, Le Corbusier. Pioneering manifesto by founder of "International School." Technical and aesthetic theories, views of industry, economics, relation of form to function, "mass-production split" and much more. Profusely illustrated. 320pp. 6⅛ x 9¼. (Available in U.S. only.) 0-486-25023-7

HOW THE OTHER HALF LIVES, Jacob Riis. Famous journalistic record, exposing poverty and degradation of New York slums around 1900, by major social reformer. 100 striking and influential photographs. 233pp. 10 x 7⅞. 0-486-22012-5

FRUIT KEY AND TWIG KEY TO TREES AND SHRUBS, William M. Harlow. One of the handiest and most widely used identification aids. Fruit key covers 120 deciduous and evergreen species; twig key 160 deciduous species. Easily used. Over 300 photographs. 126pp. 5⅜ x 8½. 0-486-20511-8

COMMON BIRD SONGS, Dr. Donald J. Borror. Songs of 60 most common U.S. birds: robins, sparrows, cardinals, bluejays, finches, more–arranged in order of increasing complexity. Up to 9 variations of songs of each species. Cassette and manual 0-486-99911-4

ORCHIDS AS HOUSE PLANTS, Rebecca Tyson Northen. Grow cattleyas and many other kinds of orchids–in a window, in a case, or under artificial light. 63 illustrations. 148pp. 5⅜ x 8½. 0-486-23261-1

MONSTER MAZES, Dave Phillips. Masterful mazes at four levels of difficulty. Avoid deadly perils and evil creatures to find magical treasures. Solutions for all 32 exciting illustrated puzzles. 48pp. 8¼ x 11. 0-486-26005-4

MOZART'S DON GIOVANNI (DOVER OPERA LIBRETTO SERIES), Wolfgang Amadeus Mozart. Introduced and translated by Ellen H. Bleiler. Standard Italian libretto, with complete English translation. Convenient and thoroughly portable–an ideal companion for reading along with a recording or the performance itself. Introduction. List of characters. Plot summary. 121pp. 5¼ x 8½. 0-486-24944-1

FRANK LLOYD WRIGHT'S DANA HOUSE, Donald Hoffmann. Pictorial essay of residential masterpiece with over 160 interior and exterior photos, plans, elevations, sketches and studies. 128pp. 9¼ x 10¾. 0-486-29120-0

THE CLARINET AND CLARINET PLAYING, David Pino. Lively, comprehensive work features suggestions about technique, musicianship, and musical interpretation, as well as guidelines for teaching, making your own reeds, and preparing for public performance. Includes an intriguing look at clarinet history. "A godsend," *The Clarinet,* Journal of the International Clarinet Society. Appendixes. 7 illus. 320pp. $5\frac{3}{8}$ x $8\frac{1}{2}$. 0-486-40270-3

HOLLYWOOD GLAMOR PORTRAITS, John Kobal (ed.). 145 photos from 1926-49. Harlow, Gable, Bogart, Bacall; 94 stars in all. Full background on photographers, technical aspects. 160pp. $8\frac{3}{8}$ x $11\frac{1}{4}$. 0-486-23352-9

THE RAVEN AND OTHER FAVORITE POEMS, Edgar Allan Poe. Over 40 of the author's most memorable poems: "The Bells," "Ulalume," "Israfel," "To Helen," "The Conqueror Worm," "Eldorado," "Annabel Lee," many more. Alphabetic lists of titles and first lines. 64pp. $5\frac{3}{16}$ x $8\frac{1}{4}$. 0-486-26685-0

PERSONAL MEMOIRS OF U. S. GRANT, Ulysses Simpson Grant. Intelligent, deeply moving firsthand account of Civil War campaigns, considered by many the finest military memoirs ever written. Includes letters, historic photographs, maps and more. 528pp. $6\frac{1}{8}$ x $9\frac{1}{4}$. 0-486-28587-1

ANCIENT EGYPTIAN MATERIALS AND INDUSTRIES, A. Lucas and J. Harris. Fascinating, comprehensive, thoroughly documented text describes this ancient civilization's vast resources and the processes that incorporated them in daily life, including the use of animal products, building materials, cosmetics, perfumes and incense, fibers, glazed ware, glass and its manufacture, materials used in the mummification process, and much more. 544pp. $6\frac{1}{8}$ x $9\frac{1}{4}$. (Available in U.S. only.) 0-486-40446-3

RUSSIAN STORIES/RUSSKIE RASSKAZY: A Dual-Language Book, edited by Gleb Struve. Twelve tales by such masters as Chekhov, Tolstoy, Dostoevsky, Pushkin, others. Excellent word-for-word English translations on facing pages, plus teaching and study aids, Russian/English vocabulary, biographical/critical introductions, more. 416pp. $5\frac{3}{8}$ x $8\frac{1}{2}$. 0-486-26244-8

PHILADELPHIA THEN AND NOW: 60 Sites Photographed in the Past and Present, Kenneth Finkel and Susan Oyama. Rare photographs of City Hall, Logan Square, Independence Hall, Betsy Ross House, other landmarks juxtaposed with contemporary views. Captures changing face of historic city. Introduction. Captions. 128pp. $8\frac{1}{4}$ x 11. 0-486-25790-8

NORTH AMERICAN INDIAN LIFE: Customs and Traditions of 23 Tribes, Elsie Clews Parsons (ed.). 27 fictionalized essays by noted anthropologists examine religion, customs, government, additional facets of life among the Winnebago, Crow, Zuni, Eskimo, other tribes. 480pp. $6\frac{1}{8}$ x $9\frac{1}{4}$. 0-486-27377-6

TECHNICAL MANUAL AND DICTIONARY OF CLASSICAL BALLET, Gail Grant. Defines, explains, comments on steps, movements, poses and concepts. 15-page pictorial section. Basic book for student, viewer. 127pp. $5\frac{3}{8}$ x $8\frac{1}{2}$. 0-486-21843-0

THE MALE AND FEMALE FIGURE IN MOTION: 60 Classic Photographic Sequences, Eadweard Muybridge. 60 true-action photographs of men and women walking, running, climbing, bending, turning, etc., reproduced from rare 19th-century masterpiece. vi + 121pp. 9 x 12. 0-486-24745-7

# CATALOG OF DOVER BOOKS

ANIMALS: 1,419 Copyright-Free Illustrations of Mammals, Birds, Fish, Insects, etc., Jim Harter (ed.). Clear wood engravings present, in extremely lifelike poses, over 1,000 species of animals. One of the most extensive pictorial sourcebooks of its kind. Captions. Index. 284pp. 9 x 12. 0-486-23766-4

1001 QUESTIONS ANSWERED ABOUT THE SEASHORE, N. J. Berrill and Jacquelyn Berrill. Queries answered about dolphins, sea snails, sponges, starfish, fishes, shore birds, many others. Covers appearance, breeding, growth, feeding, much more. 305pp. 5¼ x 8¼. 0-486-23366-9

ATTRACTING BIRDS TO YOUR YARD, William J. Weber. Easy-to-follow guide offers advice on how to attract the greatest diversity of birds: birdhouses, feeders, water and waterers, much more. 96pp. 5³⁄₁₆ x 8¼. 0-486-28927-3

MEDICINAL AND OTHER USES OF NORTH AMERICAN PLANTS: A Historical Survey with Special Reference to the Eastern Indian Tribes, Charlotte Erichsen-Brown. Chronological historical citations document 500 years of usage of plants, trees, shrubs native to eastern Canada, northeastern U.S. Also complete identifying information. 343 illustrations. 544pp. 6½ x 9¼. 0-486-25951-X

STORYBOOK MAZES, Dave Phillips. 23 stories and mazes on two-page spreads: Wizard of Oz, Treasure Island, Robin Hood, etc. Solutions. 64pp. 8¼ x 11. 0-486-23628-5

AMERICAN NEGRO SONGS: 230 Folk Songs and Spirituals, Religious and Secular, John W. Work. This authoritative study traces the African influences of songs sung and played by black Americans at work, in church, and as entertainment. The author discusses the lyric significance of such songs as "Swing Low, Sweet Chariot," "John Henry," and others and offers the words and music for 230 songs. Bibliography. Index of Song Titles. 272pp. 6½ x 9¼. 0-486-40271-1

MOVIE-STAR PORTRAITS OF THE FORTIES, John Kobal (ed.). 163 glamor, studio photos of 106 stars of the 1940s: Rita Hayworth, Ava Gardner, Marlon Brando, Clark Gable, many more. 176pp. 8⅜ x 11¼. 0-486-23546-7

YEKL and THE IMPORTED BRIDEGROOM AND OTHER STORIES OF YIDDISH NEW YORK, Abraham Cahan. Film Hester Street based on *Yekl* (1896). Novel, other stories among first about Jewish immigrants on N.Y.'s East Side. 240pp. 5⅜ x 8½. 0-486-22427-9

SELECTED POEMS, Walt Whitman. Generous sampling from *Leaves of Grass*. Twenty-four poems include "I Hear America Singing," "Song of the Open Road," "I Sing the Body Electric," "When Lilacs Last in the Dooryard Bloom'd," "O Captain! My Captain!"—all reprinted from an authoritative edition. Lists of titles and first lines. 128pp. 5³⁄₁₆ x 8¼. 0-486-26878-0

SONGS OF EXPERIENCE: Facsimile Reproduction with 26 Plates in Full Color, William Blake. 26 full-color plates from a rare 1826 edition. Includes "The Tyger," "London," "Holy Thursday," and other poems. Printed text of poems. 48pp. 5¼ x 7. 0-486-24636-1

THE BEST TALES OF HOFFMANN, E. T. A. Hoffmann. 10 of Hoffmann's most important stories: "Nutcracker and the King of Mice," "The Golden Flowerpot," etc. 458pp. 5⅜ x 8½. 0-486-21793-0

THE BOOK OF TEA, Kakuzo Okakura. Minor classic of the Orient: entertaining, charming explanation, interpretation of traditional Japanese culture in terms of tea ceremony. 94pp. 5⅜ x 8½. 0-486-20070-1

FRENCH STORIES/CONTES FRANÇAIS: A Dual-Language Book, Wallace Fowlie. Ten stories by French masters, Voltaire to Camus: "Micromegas" by Voltaire; "The Atheist's Mass" by Balzac; "Minuet" by de Maupassant; "The Guest" by Camus, six more. Excellent English translations on facing pages. Also French-English vocabulary list, exercises, more. 352pp. 5⅜ x 8½. 0-486-26443-2

CHICAGO AT THE TURN OF THE CENTURY IN PHOTOGRAPHS: 122 Historic Views from the Collections of the Chicago Historical Society, Larry A. Viskochil. Rare large-format prints offer detailed views of City Hall, State Street, the Loop, Hull House, Union Station, many other landmarks, circa 1904-1913. Introduction. Captions. Maps. 144pp. 9⅜ x 12¼. 0-486-24656-6

OLD BROOKLYN IN EARLY PHOTOGRAPHS, 1865-1929, William Lee Younger. Luna Park, Gravesend race track, construction of Grand Army Plaza, moving of Hotel Brighton, etc. 157 previously unpublished photographs. 165pp. 8⅞ x 11¾. 0-486-23587-4

THE MYTHS OF THE NORTH AMERICAN INDIANS, Lewis Spence. Rich anthology of the myths and legends of the Algonquins, Iroquois, Pawnees and Sioux, prefaced by an extensive historical and ethnological commentary. 36 illustrations. 480pp. 5⅜ x 8½. 0-486-25967-6

AN ENCYCLOPEDIA OF BATTLES: Accounts of Over 1,560 Battles from 1479 B.C. to the Present, David Eggenberger. Essential details of every major battle in recorded history from the first battle of Megiddo in 1479 B.C. to Grenada in 1984. List of Battle Maps. New Appendix covering the years 1967-1984. Index. 99 illustrations. 544pp. 6½ x 9¼. 0-486-24913-1

SAILING ALONE AROUND THE WORLD, Captain Joshua Slocum. First man to sail around the world, alone, in small boat. One of great feats of seamanship told in delightful manner. 67 illustrations. 294pp. 5⅜ x 8½. 0-486-20326-3

ANARCHISM AND OTHER ESSAYS, Emma Goldman. Powerful, penetrating, prophetic essays on direct action, role of minorities, prison reform, puritan hypocrisy, violence, etc. 271pp. 5⅜ x 8½. 0-486-22484-8

MYTHS OF THE HINDUS AND BUDDHISTS, Ananda K. Coomaraswamy and Sister Nivedita. Great stories of the epics; deeds of Krishna, Shiva, taken from puranas, Vedas, folk tales; etc. 32 illustrations. 400pp. 5⅜ x 8½. 0-486-21759-0

MY BONDAGE AND MY FREEDOM, Frederick Douglass. Born a slave, Douglass became outspoken force in antislavery movement. The best of Douglass' autobiographies. Graphic description of slave life. 464pp. 5⅜ x 8½. 0-486-22457-0

FOLLOWING THE EQUATOR: A Journey Around the World, Mark Twain. Fascinating humorous account of 1897 voyage to Hawaii, Australia, India, New Zealand, etc. Ironic, bemused reports on peoples, customs, climate, flora and fauna, politics, much more. 197 illustrations. 720pp. 5⅜ x 8½. 0-486-26113-1

THE PEOPLE CALLED SHAKERS, Edward D. Andrews. Definitive study of Shakers: origins, beliefs, practices, dances, social organization, furniture and crafts, etc. 33 illustrations. 351pp. 5⅜ x 8½. 0-486-21081-2

THE MYTHS OF GREECE AND ROME, H. A. Guerber. A classic of mythology, generously illustrated, long prized for its simple, graphic, accurate retelling of the principal myths of Greece and Rome, and for its commentary on their origins and significance. With 64 illustrations by Michelangelo, Raphael, Titian, Rubens, Canova, Bernini and others. 480pp. 5⅜ x 8½. 0-486-27584-1

# CATALOG OF DOVER BOOKS

PSYCHOLOGY OF MUSIC, Carl E. Seashore. Classic work discusses music as a medium from psychological viewpoint. Clear treatment of physical acoustics, auditory apparatus, sound perception, development of musical skills, nature of musical feeling, host of other topics. 88 figures. 408pp. 5⅜ x 8½. 0-486-21851-1

LIFE IN ANCIENT EGYPT, Adolf Erman. Fullest, most thorough, detailed older account with much not in more recent books, domestic life, religion, magic, medicine, commerce, much more. Many illustrations reproduce tomb paintings, carvings, hieroglyphs, etc. 597pp. 5⅜ x 8½. 0-486-22632-8

SUNDIALS, Their Theory and Construction, Albert Waugh. Far and away the best, most thorough coverage of ideas, mathematics concerned, types, construction, adjusting anywhere. Simple, nontechnical treatment allows even children to build several of these dials. Over 100 illustrations. 230pp. 5⅜ x 8½. 0-486-22947-5

THEORETICAL HYDRODYNAMICS, L. M. Milne-Thomson. Classic exposition of the mathematical theory of fluid motion, applicable to both hydrodynamics and aerodynamics. Over 600 exercises. 768pp. 6⅛ x 9¼. 0-486-68970-0

OLD-TIME VIGNETTES IN FULL COLOR, Carol Belanger Grafton (ed.). Over 390 charming, often sentimental illustrations, selected from archives of Victorian graphics–pretty women posing, children playing, food, flowers, kittens and puppies, smiling cherubs, birds and butterflies, much more. All copyright-free. 48pp. 9¼ x 12¼. 0-486-27269-9

PERSPECTIVE FOR ARTISTS, Rex Vicat Cole. Depth, perspective of sky and sea, shadows, much more, not usually covered. 391 diagrams, 81 reproductions of drawings and paintings. 279pp. 5⅜ x 8½. 0-486-22487-2

DRAWING THE LIVING FIGURE, Joseph Sheppard. Innovative approach to artistic anatomy focuses on specifics of surface anatomy, rather than muscles and bones. Over 170 drawings of live models in front, back and side views, and in widely varying poses. Accompanying diagrams. 177 illustrations. Introduction. Index. 144pp. 8⅜ x11¼. 0-486-26723-7

GOTHIC AND OLD ENGLISH ALPHABETS: 100 Complete Fonts, Dan X. Solo. Add power, elegance to posters, signs, other graphics with 100 stunning copyright-free alphabets: Blackstone, Dolbey, Germania, 97 more–including many lower-case, numerals, punctuation marks. 104pp. 8⅛ x 11. 0-486-24695-7

THE BOOK OF WOOD CARVING, Charles Marshall Sayers. Finest book for beginners discusses fundamentals and offers 34 designs. "Absolutely first rate . . . well thought out and well executed."–E. J. Tangerman. 118pp. 7¾ x 10⅝. 0-486-23654-4

ILLUSTRATED CATALOG OF CIVIL WAR MILITARY GOODS: Union Army Weapons, Insignia, Uniform Accessories, and Other Equipment, Schuyler, Hartley, and Graham. Rare, profusely illustrated 1846 catalog includes Union Army uniform and dress regulations, arms and ammunition, coats, insignia, flags, swords, rifles, etc. 226 illustrations. 160pp. 9 x 12. 0-486-24939-5

WOMEN'S FASHIONS OF THE EARLY 1900s: An Unabridged Republication of "New York Fashions, 1909," National Cloak & Suit Co. Rare catalog of mail-order fashions documents women's and children's clothing styles shortly after the turn of the century. Captions offer full descriptions, prices. Invaluable resource for fashion, costume historians. Approximately 725 illustrations. 128pp. 8⅜ x 11¼.

0-486-27276-1

HOW TO DO BEADWORK, Mary White. Fundamental book on craft from simple projects to five-bead chains and woven works. 106 illustrations. 142pp. 5⅜ x 8.
0-486-20697-1

THE 1912 AND 1915 GUSTAV STICKLEY FURNITURE CATALOGS, Gustav Stickley. With over 200 detailed illustrations and descriptions, these two catalogs are essential reading and reference materials and identification guides for Stickley furniture. Captions cite materials, dimensions and prices. 112pp. 6½ x 9¼. 0-486-26676-1

EARLY AMERICAN LOCOMOTIVES, John H. White, Jr. Finest locomotive engravings from early 19th century: historical (1804–74), main-line (after 1870), special, foreign, etc. 147 plates. 142pp. 11⅜ x 8¼. 0-486-22772-3

LITTLE BOOK OF EARLY AMERICAN CRAFTS AND TRADES, Peter Stockham (ed.). 1807 children's book explains crafts and trades: baker, hatter, cooper, potter, and many others. 23 copperplate illustrations. 140pp. 4⅝ x 6.
0-486-23336-7

VICTORIAN FASHIONS AND COSTUMES FROM HARPER'S BAZAR, 1867–1898, Stella Blum (ed.). Day costumes, evening wear, sports clothes, shoes, hats, other accessories in over 1,000 detailed engravings. 320pp. 9⅜ x 12¼.
0-486-22990-4

THE LONG ISLAND RAIL ROAD IN EARLY PHOTOGRAPHS, Ron Ziel. Over 220 rare photos, informative text document origin ( 1844) and development of rail service on Long Island. Vintage views of early trains, locomotives, stations, passengers, crews, much more. Captions. 8⅞ x 11¾. 0-486-26301-0

VOYAGE OF THE LIBERDADE, Joshua Slocum. Great 19th-century mariner's thrilling, first-hand account of the wreck of his ship off South America, the 35-foot boat he built from the wreckage, and its remarkable voyage home. 128pp. 5⅜ x 8½.
0-486-40022-0

TEN BOOKS ON ARCHITECTURE, Vitruvius. The most important book ever written on architecture. Early Roman aesthetics, technology, classical orders, site selection, all other aspects. Morgan translation. 331pp. 5⅜ x 8½. 0-486-20645-9

THE HUMAN FIGURE IN MOTION, Eadweard Muybridge. More than 4,500 stopped-action photos, in action series, showing undraped men, women, children jumping, lying down, throwing, sitting, wrestling, carrying, etc. 390pp. 7⅞ x 10⅝.
0-486-20204-6 Clothbd.

TREES OF THE EASTERN AND CENTRAL UNITED STATES AND CANADA, William M. Harlow. Best one-volume guide to 140 trees. Full descriptions, woodlore, range, etc. Over 600 illustrations. Handy size. 288pp. 4½ x 6⅜. 0-486-20395-6

GROWING AND USING HERBS AND SPICES, Milo Miloradovich. Versatile handbook provides all the information needed for cultivation and use of all the herbs and spices available in North America. 4 illustrations. Index. Glossary. 236pp. 5⅜ x 8½.
0-486-25058-X

BIG BOOK OF MAZES AND LABYRINTHS, Walter Shepherd. 50 mazes and labyrinths in all–classical, solid, ripple, and more–in one great volume. Perfect inexpensive puzzler for clever youngsters. Full solutions. 112pp. 8⅛ x 11. 0-486-22951-3

PIANO TUNING, J. Cree Fischer. Clearest, best book for beginner, amateur. Simple repairs, raising dropped notes, tuning by easy method of flattened fifths. No previous skills needed. 4 illustrations. 201pp. 5⅜ x 8½. 0-486-23267-0

HINTS TO SINGERS, Lillian Nordica. Selecting the right teacher, developing confidence, overcoming stage fright, and many other important skills receive thoughtful discussion in this indispensible guide, written by a world-famous diva of four decades' experience. 96pp. 5⅜ x 8½. 0-486-40094-8

THE COMPLETE NONSENSE OF EDWARD LEAR, Edward Lear. All nonsense limericks, zany alphabets, Owl and Pussycat, songs, nonsense botany, etc., illustrated by Lear. Total of 320pp. 5⅜ x 8½. (Available in U.S. only.) 0-486-20167-8

VICTORIAN PARLOUR POETRY: An Annotated Anthology, Michael R. Turner. 117 gems by Longfellow, Tennyson, Browning, many lesser-known poets. "The Village Blacksmith," "Curfew Must Not Ring Tonight," "Only a Baby Small," dozens more, often difficult to find elsewhere. Index of poets, titles, first lines. xxiii + 325pp. 5⅝ x 8¼. 0-486-27044-0

DUBLINERS, James Joyce. Fifteen stories offer vivid, tightly focused observations of the lives of Dublin's poorer classes. At least one, "The Dead," is considered a masterpiece. Reprinted complete and unabridged from standard edition. 160pp. 5 3/16 x 8¼. 0-486-26870-5

GREAT WEIRD TALES: 14 Stories by Lovecraft, Blackwood, Machen and Others, S. T. Joshi (ed.). 14 spellbinding tales, including "The Sin Eater," by Fiona McLeod, "The Eye Above the Mantel," by Frank Belknap Long, as well as renowned works by R. H. Barlow, Lord Dunsany, Arthur Machen, W. C. Morrow and eight other masters of the genre. 256pp. 5⅜ x 8½. (Available in U.S. only.) 0-486-40436-6

THE BOOK OF THE SACRED MAGIC OF ABRAMELIN THE MAGE, translated by S. MacGregor Mathers. Medieval manuscript of ceremonial magic. Basic document in Aleister Crowley, Golden Dawn groups. 268pp. 5⅜ x 8½. 0-486-23211-5

THE BATTLES THAT CHANGED HISTORY, Fletcher Pratt. Eminent historian profiles 16 crucial conflicts, ancient to modern, that changed the course of civilization. 352pp. 5⅜ x 8½. 0-486-41129-X

NEW RUSSIAN-ENGLISH AND ENGLISH-RUSSIAN DICTIONARY, M. A. O'Brien. This is a remarkably handy Russian dictionary, containing a surprising amount of information, including over 70,000 entries. 366pp. 4½ x 6⅛. 0-486-20208-9

NEW YORK IN THE FORTIES, Andreas Feininger. 162 brilliant photographs by the well-known photographer, formerly with *Life* magazine. Commuters, shoppers, Times Square at night, much else from city at its peak. Captions by John von Hartz. 181pp. 9¼ x 10¾. 0-486-23585-8

INDIAN SIGN LANGUAGE, William Tomkins. Over 525 signs developed by Sioux and other tribes. Written instructions and diagrams. Also 290 pictographs. 111pp. 6⅛ x 9¼. 0-486-22029-X

ANATOMY: A Complete Guide for Artists, Joseph Sheppard. A master of figure drawing shows artists how to render human anatomy convincingly. Over 460 illustrations. 224pp. 8⅜ x 11¼. 0-486-27279-6

MEDIEVAL CALLIGRAPHY: Its History and Technique, Marc Drogin. Spirited history, comprehensive instruction manual covers 13 styles (ca. 4th century through 15th). Excellent photographs; directions for duplicating medieval techniques with modern tools. 224pp. 8⅜ x 11¼. 0-486-26142-5

CATALOG OF DOVER BOOKS

DRIED FLOWERS: How to Prepare Them, Sarah Whitlock and Martha Rankin.
Complete instructions on how to use silica gel, meal and borax, perlite aggregate,
sand and borax, glycerine and water to create attractive permanent flower arrange-
ments. 12 illustrations. 32pp. 5⅜ x 8½.                      0-486-21802-3

EASY-TO-MAKE BIRD FEEDERS FOR WOODWORKERS, Scott D. Campbell.
Detailed, simple-to-use guide for designing, constructing, caring for and using feeders. Text, illustrations for 12 classic and contemporary designs. 96pp. 5⅜ x 8½.
                                                            0-486-25847-5

THE COMPLETE BOOK OF BIRDHOUSE CONSTRUCTION FOR WOOD-
WORKERS, Scott D. Campbell. Detailed instructions, illustrations, tables. Also data
on bird habitat and instinct patterns. Bibliography. 3 tables. 63 illustrations in 15 figures. 48pp. 5¼ x 8½.                                        0-486-24407-5

SCOTTISH WONDER TALES FROM MYTH AND LEGEND, Donald A.
Mackenzie. 16 lively tales tell of giants rumbling down mountainsides, of a magic
wand that turns stone pillars into warriors, of gods and goddesses, evil hags, powerful forces and more. 240pp. 5⅜ x 8½.                        0-486-29677-6

THE HISTORY OF UNDERCLOTHES, C. Willett Cunnington and Phyllis
Cunnington. Fascinating, well-documented survey covering six centuries of English
undergarments, enhanced with over 100 illustrations: 12th-century laced-up bodice,
footed long drawers (1795), 19th-century bustles, l9th-century corsets for men,
Victorian "bust improvers," much more. 272pp. 5⅜ x 8¼.      0-486-27124-2

ARTS AND CRAFTS FURNITURE: The Complete Brooks Catalog of 1912,
Brooks Manufacturing Co. Photos and detailed descriptions of more than 150 now
very collectible furniture designs from the Arts and Crafts movement depict daven-
ports, settees, buffets, desks, tables, chairs, bedsteads, dressers and more, all built of
solid, quarter-sawed oak. Invaluable for students and enthusiasts of antiques,
Americana and the decorative arts. 80pp. 6½ x 9¼.           0-486-27471-3

WILBUR AND ORVILLE: A Biography of the Wright Brothers, Fred Howard.
Definitive, crisply written study tells the full story of the brothers' lives and work. A
vividly written biography, unparalleled in scope and color, that also captures the
spirit of an extraordinary era. 560pp. 6⅛ x 9¼.             0-486-40297-5

THE ARTS OF THE SAILOR: Knotting, Splicing and Ropework, Hervey Garrett
Smith. Indispensable shipboard reference covers tools, basic knots and useful hitches;
handsewing and canvas work, more. Over 100 illustrations. Delightful reading for sea
lovers. 256pp. 5⅜ x 8½.                                     0-486-26440-8

FRANK LLOYD WRIGHT'S FALLINGWATER: The House and Its History,
Second, Revised Edition, Donald Hoffmann. A total revision–both in text and illustrations–of the standard document on Fallingwater, the boldest, most personal architectural statement of Wright's mature years, updated with valuable new material
from the recently opened Frank Lloyd Wright Archives. "Fascinating"–*The New York
Times.* 116 illustrations. 128pp. 9¾ x 10¾.                 0-486-27430-6

PHOTOGRAPHIC SKETCHBOOK OF THE CIVIL WAR, Alexander Gardner.
100 photos taken on field during the Civil War. Famous shots of Manassas Harper's
Ferry, Lincoln, Richmond, slave pens, etc. 244pp. 10⅝ x 8¼.  0-486-22731-6

FIVE ACRES AND INDEPENDENCE, Maurice G. Kains. Great back-to-the-land
classic explains basics of self-sufficient farming. The one book to get. 95 illustrations.
397pp. 5⅜ x 8½.                                             0-486-20974-1

# CATALOG OF DOVER BOOKS

A MODERN HERBAL, Margaret Grieve. Much the fullest, most exact, most useful compilation of herbal material. Gigantic alphabetical encyclopedia, from aconite to zedoary, gives botanical information, medical properties, folklore, economic uses, much else. Indispensable to serious reader. 161 illustrations. 888pp. 6½ x 9¼. 2-vol. set. (Available in U.S. only.) Vol. I: 0-486-22798-7 Vol. II: 0-486-22799-5

HIDDEN TREASURE MAZE BOOK, Dave Phillips. Solve 34 challenging mazes accompanied by heroic tales of adventure. Evil dragons, people-eating plants, blood-thirsty giants, many more dangerous adversaries lurk at every twist and turn. 34 mazes, stories, solutions. 48pp. 8¼ x 11. 0-486-24566-7

LETTERS OF W. A. MOZART, Wolfgang A. Mozart. Remarkable letters show bawdy wit, humor, imagination, musical insights, contemporary musical world; includes some letters from Leopold Mozart. 276pp. 5⅜ x 8½. 0-486-22859-2

BASIC PRINCIPLES OF CLASSICAL BALLET, Agrippina Vaganova. Great Russian theoretician, teacher explains methods for teaching classical ballet. 118 illustrations. 175pp. 5⅜ x 8½. 0-486-22036-2

THE JUMPING FROG, Mark Twain. Revenge edition. The original story of The Celebrated Jumping Frog of Calaveras County, a hapless French translation, and Twain's hilarious "retranslation" from the French. 12 illustrations. 66pp. 5⅜ x 8½. 0-486-22686-7

BEST REMEMBERED POEMS, Martin Gardner (ed.). The 126 poems in this superb collection of 19th- and 20th-century British and American verse range from Shelley's "To a Skylark" to the impassioned "Renascence" of Edna St. Vincent Millay and to Edward Lear's whimsical "The Owl and the Pussycat." 224pp. 5⅜ x 8½. 0-486-27165-X

COMPLETE SONNETS, William Shakespeare. Over 150 exquisite poems deal with love, friendship, the tyranny of time, beauty's evanescence, death and other themes in language of remarkable power, precision and beauty. Glossary of archaic terms. 80pp. 5³⁄₁₆ x 8¼. 0-486-26686-9

HISTORIC HOMES OF THE AMERICAN PRESIDENTS, Second, Revised Edition, Irvin Haas. A traveler's guide to American Presidential homes, most open to the public, depicting and describing homes occupied by every American President from George Washington to George Bush. With visiting hours, admission charges, travel routes. 175 photographs. Index. 160pp. 8¼ x 11. 0-486-26751-2

THE WIT AND HUMOR OF OSCAR WILDE, Alvin Redman (ed.). More than 1,000 ripostes, paradoxes, wisecracks: Work is the curse of the drinking classes; I can resist everything except temptation; etc. 258pp. 5⅜ x 8½. 0-486-20602-5

SHAKESPEARE LEXICON AND QUOTATION DICTIONARY, Alexander Schmidt. Full definitions, locations, shades of meaning in every word in plays and poems. More than 50,000 exact quotations. 1,485pp. 6½ x 9¼. 2-vol. set.
Vol. 1: 0-486-22726-X Vol. 2: 0-486-22727-8

SELECTED POEMS, Emily Dickinson. Over 100 best-known, best-loved poems by one of America's foremost poets, reprinted from authoritative early editions. No comparable edition at this price. Index of first lines. 64pp. 5³⁄₁₆ x 8¼. 0-486-26466-1

THE INSIDIOUS DR. FU-MANCHU, Sax Rohmer. The first of the popular mystery series introduces a pair of English detectives to their archnemesis, the diabolical Dr. Fu-Manchu. Flavorful atmosphere, fast-paced action, and colorful characters enliven this classic of the genre. 208pp. 5³⁄₁₆ x 8¼. 0-486-29898-1

THE MALLEUS MALEFICARUM OF KRAMER AND SPRENGER, translated by Montague Summers. Full text of most important witchhunter's "bible," used by both Catholics and Protestants. 278pp. 6⅝ x 10. 0-486-22802-9

SPANISH STORIES/CUENTOS ESPAÑOLES: A Dual-Language Book, Angel Flores (ed.). Unique format offers 13 great stories in Spanish by Cervantes, Borges, others. Faithful English translations on facing pages. 352pp. 5⅜ x 8½. 0-486-25399-6

GARDEN CITY, LONG ISLAND, IN EARLY PHOTOGRAPHS, 1869–1919, Mildred H. Smith. Handsome treasury of 118 vintage pictures, accompanied by carefully researched captions, document the Garden City Hotel fire (1899), the Vanderbilt Cup Race (1908), the first airmail flight departing from the Nassau Boulevard Aerodrome (1911), and much more. 96pp. 8⅞ x 11¾. 0-486-40669-5

OLD QUEENS, N.Y., IN EARLY PHOTOGRAPHS, Vincent F. Seyfried and William Asadorian. Over 160 rare photographs of Maspeth, Jamaica, Jackson Heights, and other areas. Vintage views of DeWitt Clinton mansion, 1939 World's Fair and more. Captions. 192pp. 8⅞ x 11. 0-486-26358-4

CAPTURED BY THE INDIANS: 15 Firsthand Accounts, 1750-1870, Frederick Drimmer. Astounding true historical accounts of grisly torture, bloody conflicts, relentless pursuits, miraculous escapes and more, by people who lived to tell the tale. 384pp. 5⅜ x 8½. 0-486-24901-8

THE WORLD'S GREAT SPEECHES (Fourth Enlarged Edition), Lewis Copeland, Lawrence W. Lamm, and Stephen J. McKenna. Nearly 300 speeches provide public speakers with a wealth of updated quotes and inspiration–from Pericles' funeral oration and William Jennings Bryan's "Cross of Gold Speech" to Malcolm X's powerful words on the Black Revolution and Earl of Spenser's tribute to his sister, Diana, Princess of Wales. 944pp. 5⅜ x 8⅜. 0-486-40903-1

THE BOOK OF THE SWORD, Sir Richard F. Burton. Great Victorian scholar/adventurer's eloquent, erudite history of the "queen of weapons"–from prehistory to early Roman Empire. Evolution and development of early swords, variations (sabre, broadsword, cutlass, scimitar, etc.), much more. 336pp. 6⅛ x 9¼. 0-486-25434-8

AUTOBIOGRAPHY: The Story of My Experiments with Truth, Mohandas K. Gandhi. Boyhood, legal studies, purification, the growth of the Satyagraha (nonviolent protest) movement. Critical, inspiring work of the man responsible for the freedom of India. 480pp. 5⅜ x 8½. (Available in U.S. only.) 0-486-24593-4

CELTIC MYTHS AND LEGENDS, T. W. Rolleston. Masterful retelling of Irish and Welsh stories and tales. Cuchulain, King Arthur, Deirdre, the Grail, many more. First paperback edition. 58 full-page illustrations. 512pp. 5⅜ x 8½. 0-486-26507-2

THE PRINCIPLES OF PSYCHOLOGY, William James. Famous long course complete, unabridged. Stream of thought, time perception, memory, experimental methods; great work decades ahead of its time. 94 figures. 1,391pp. 5⅜ x 8½. 2-vol. set. Vol. I: 0-486-20381-6 Vol. II: 0-486-20382-4

THE WORLD AS WILL AND REPRESENTATION, Arthur Schopenhauer. Definitive English translation of Schopenhauer's life work, correcting more than 1,000 errors, omissions in earlier translations. Translated by E. F. J. Payne. Total of 1,269pp. 5⅜ x 8½. 2-vol. set. Vol. 1: 0-486-21761-2 Vol. 2: 0-486-21762-0

# CATALOG OF DOVER BOOKS

MAGIC AND MYSTERY IN TIBET, Madame Alexandra David-Neel. Experiences among lamas, magicians, sages, sorcerers, Bonpa wizards. A true psychic discovery. 32 illustrations. 321pp. 5⅜ x 8½. (Available in U.S. only.) 0-486-22682-4

THE EGYPTIAN BOOK OF THE DEAD, E. A. Wallis Budge. Complete reproduction of Ani's papyrus, finest ever found. Full hieroglyphic text, interlinear transliteration, word-for-word translation, smooth translation. 533pp. 6½ x 9¼. 0-486-21866-X

HISTORIC COSTUME IN PICTURES, Braun & Schneider. Over 1,450 costumed figures in clearly detailed engravings–from dawn of civilization to end of 19th century. Captions. Many folk costumes. 256pp. 8⅜ x 11¾. 0-486-23150-X

MATHEMATICS FOR THE NONMATHEMATICIAN, Morris Kline. Detailed, college-level treatment of mathematics in cultural and historical context, with numerous exercises. Recommended Reading Lists. Tables. Numerous figures. 641pp. 5⅜ x 8½. 0-486-24823-2

PROBABILISTIC METHODS IN THE THEORY OF STRUCTURES, Isaac Elishakoff. Well-written introduction covers the elements of the theory of probability from two or more random variables, the reliability of such multivariable structures, the theory of random function, Monte Carlo methods of treating problems incapable of exact solution, and more. Examples. 502pp. 5⅜ x 8½. 0-486-40691-1

THE RIME OF THE ANCIENT MARINER, Gustave Doré, S. T. Coleridge. Doré's finest work; 34 plates capture moods, subtleties of poem. Flawless full-size reproductions printed on facing pages with authoritative text of poem. "Beautiful. Simply beautiful."–*Publisher's Weekly.* 77pp. 9¼ x 12. 0-486-22305-1

SCULPTURE: Principles and Practice, Louis Slobodkin. Step-by-step approach to clay, plaster, metals, stone; classical and modern. 253 drawings, photos. 255pp. 8⅛ x 11. 0-486-22960-2

THE INFLUENCE OF SEA POWER UPON HISTORY, 1660–1783, A. T. Mahan. Influential classic of naval history and tactics still used as text in war colleges. First paperback edition. 4 maps. 24 battle plans. 640pp. 5⅜ x 8½. 0-486-25509-3

THE STORY OF THE TITANIC AS TOLD BY ITS SURVIVORS, Jack Winocour (ed.). What it was really like. Panic, despair, shocking inefficiency, and a little heroism. More thrilling than any fictional account. 26 illustrations. 320pp. 5⅜ x 8½. 0-486-20610-6

ONE TWO THREE . . . INFINITY: Facts and Speculations of Science, George Gamow. Great physicist's fascinating, readable overview of contemporary science: number theory, relativity, fourth dimension, entropy, genes, atomic structure, much more. 128 illustrations. Index. 352pp. 5⅜ x 8½. 0-486-25664-2

DALÍ ON MODERN ART: The Cuckolds of Antiquated Modern Art, Salvador Dalí. Influential painter skewers modern art and its practitioners. Outrageous evaluations of Picasso, Cézanne, Turner, more. 15 renderings of paintings discussed. 44 calligraphic decorations by Dalí. 96pp. 5⅜ x 8½. (Available in U.S. only.) 0-486-29220-7

ANTIQUE PLAYING CARDS: A Pictorial History, Henry René D'Allemagne. Over 900 elaborate, decorative images from rare playing cards (14th–20th centuries): Bacchus, death, dancing dogs, hunting scenes, royal coats of arms, players cheating, much more. 96pp. 9¼ x 12¼. 0-486-29265-7

# CATALOG OF DOVER BOOKS

MAKING FURNITURE MASTERPIECES: 30 Projects with Measured Drawings, Franklin H. Gottshall. Step-by-step instructions, illustrations for constructing handsome, useful pieces, among them a Sheraton desk, Chippendale chair, Spanish desk, Queen Anne table and a William and Mary dressing mirror. 224pp. 8⅛ x 11¼.
0-486-29338-6

NORTH AMERICAN INDIAN DESIGNS FOR ARTISTS AND CRAFTSPEOPLE, Eva Wilson. Over 360 authentic copyright-free designs adapted from Navajo blankets, Hopi pottery, Sioux buffalo hides, more. Geometrics, symbolic figures, plant and animal motifs, etc. 128pp. 8⅜ x 11. (Not for sale in the United Kingdom.)        0-486-25341-4

THE FOSSIL BOOK: A Record of Prehistoric Life, Patricia V. Rich et al. Profusely illustrated definitive guide covers everything from single-celled organisms and dinosaurs to birds and mammals and the interplay between climate and man. Over 1,500 illustrations. 760pp. 7½ x 10⅛.        0-486-29371-8

VICTORIAN ARCHITECTURAL DETAILS: Designs for Over 700 Stairs, Mantels, Doors, Windows, Cornices, Porches, and Other Decorative Elements, A. J. Bicknell & Company. Everything from dormer windows and piazzas to balconies and gable ornaments. Also includes elevations and floor plans for handsome, private residences and commercial structures. 80pp. 9⅜ x 12¼.        0-486-44015-X

WESTERN ISLAMIC ARCHITECTURE: A Concise Introduction, John D. Hoag. Profusely illustrated critical appraisal compares and contrasts Islamic mosques and palaces—from Spain and Egypt to other areas in the Middle East. 139 illustrations. 128pp. 6 x 9.        0 486-43760-4

CHINESE ARCHITECTURE: A Pictorial History, Liang Ssu-ch'eng. More than 240 rare photographs and drawings depict temples, pagodas, tombs, bridges, and imperial palaces comprising much of China's architectural heritage. 152 halftones, 94 diagrams. 232pp. 10¾ x 9⅞.        0-486-43999-2

THE RENAISSANCE: Studies in Art and Poetry, Walter Pater. One of the most talked-about books of the 19th century, *The Renaissance* combines scholarship and philosophy in an innovative work of cultural criticism that examines the achievements of Botticelli, Leonardo, Michelangelo, and other artists. "The holy writ of beauty."–Oscar Wilde. 160pp. 5⅜ x 8½.        0-486-44025-7

A TREATISE ON PAINTING, Leonardo da Vinci. The great Renaissance artist's practical advice on drawing and painting techniques covers anatomy, perspective, composition, light and shadow, and color. A classic of art instruction, it features 48 drawings by Nicholas Poussin and Leon Battista Alberti. 192pp. 5⅜ x 8½.
0-486-44155-5

THE MIND OF LEONARDO DA VINCI, Edward McCurdy. More than just a biography, this classic study by a distinguished historian draws upon Leonardo's extensive writings to offer numerous demonstrations of the Renaissance master's achievements, not only in sculpture and painting, but also in music, engineering, and even experimental aviation. 384pp. 5⅜ x 8½.        0-486-44142-3

WASHINGTON IRVING'S RIP VAN WINKLE, Illustrated by Arthur Rackham. Lovely prints that established artist as a leading illustrator of the time and forever etched into the popular imagination a classic of Catskill lore. 51 full-color plates. 80pp. 8⅜ x 11.        0-486-44242-X

HENSCHE ON PAINTING, John W. Robichaux. Basic painting philosophy and methodology of a great teacher, as expounded in his famous classes and workshops on Cape Cod. 7 illustrations in color on covers. 80pp. 5⅜ x 8½.        0-486-43728-0

LIGHT AND SHADE: A Classic Approach to Three-Dimensional Drawing, Mrs. Mary P. Merrifield. Handy reference clearly demonstrates principles of light and shade by revealing effects of common daylight, sunshine, and candle or artificial light on geometrical solids. 13 plates. 64pp. 5⅜ x 8½. 0-486-44143-1

ASTROLOGY AND ASTRONOMY: A Pictorial Archive of Signs and Symbols, Ernst and Johanna Lehner. Treasure trove of stories, lore, and myth, accompanied by more than 300 rare illustrations of planets, the Milky Way, signs of the zodiac, comets, meteors, and other astronomical phenomena. 192pp. 8⅜ x 11. 0-486-43981-X

JEWELRY MAKING: Techniques for Metal, Tim McCreight. Easy-to-follow instructions and carefully executed illustrations describe tools and techniques, use of gems and enamels, wire inlay, casting, and other topics. 72 line illustrations and diagrams. 176pp. 8¼ x 10⅞. 0-486-44043-5

MAKING BIRDHOUSES: Easy and Advanced Projects, Gladstone Califf. Easy-to-follow instructions include diagrams for everything from a one-room house for bluebirds to a forty-two-room structure for purple martins. 56 plates; 4 figures. 80pp. 8¾ x 6⅜. 0-486-44183-0

LITTLE BOOK OF LOG CABINS: How to Build and Furnish Them, William S. Wicks. Handy how-to manual, with instructions and illustrations for building cabins in the Adirondack style, fireplaces, stairways, furniture, beamed ceilings, and more. 102 line drawings. 96pp. 8¾ x 6⅜. 0-486-44259-4

THE SEASONS OF AMERICA PAST, Eric Sloane. From "sugaring time" and strawberry picking to Indian summer and fall harvest, a whole year's activities described in charming prose and enhanced with 79 of the author's own illustrations. 160pp. 8¼ x 11. 0-486-44220-9

THE METROPOLIS OF TOMORROW, Hugh Ferriss. Generous, prophetic vision of the metropolis of the future, as perceived in 1929. Powerful illustrations of towering structures, wide avenues, and rooftop parks–all features in many of today's modern cities. 59 illustrations. 144pp. 8¼ x 11. 0-486-43727-2

THE PATH TO ROME, Hilaire Belloc. This 1902 memoir abounds in lively vignettes from a vanished time, recounting a pilgrimage on foot across the Alps and Apennines in order to "see all Europe which the Christian Faith has saved." 77 of the author's original line drawings complement his sparkling prose. 272pp. 5⅜ x 8½. 0-486-44001-X

THE HISTORY OF RASSELAS: Prince of Abissinia, Samuel Johnson. Distinguished English writer attacks eighteenth-century optimism and man's unrealistic estimates of what life has to offer. 112pp. 5⅜ x 8½. 0-486-44094-X

A VOYAGE TO ARCTURUS, David Lindsay. A brilliant flight of pure fancy, where wild creatures crowd the fantastic landscape and demented torturers dominate victims with their bizarre mental powers. 272pp. 5⅜ x 8½. 0-486-44198-9

Paperbound unless otherwise indicated. Available at your book dealer, online at **www.doverpublications.com**, or by writing to Dept. GI, Dover Publications, Inc., 31 East 2nd Street, Mineola, NY 11501. For current price information or for free catalogs (please indicate field of interest), write to Dover Publications or log on to **www.doverpublications.com** and see every Dover book in print. Dover publishes more than 500 books each year on science, elementary and advanced mathematics, biology, music, art, literary history, social sciences, and other areas.